# VAMPS

# VAMPS

## An Illustrated History of the Femme Fatale

by Pam Keesey

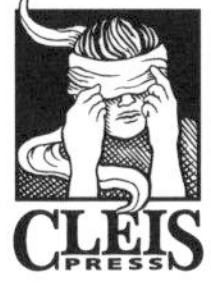

Library of Congress Cataloging-in-Publication Data

Keesey, Pam. 1964–
Vamps: an Illustrated History of the Femme Fatale/by Pam Keesey
p. cm.
Includes bibliographical references and index.
ISBN 1-57344-026-4 (pbk.)
1. Femmes fatales–History. 2. Femmes fatales in art.
3. Femmes fatales in motion pictures. 4. Femmes fatales in literature.
HO1154.K375 1997 97-38082
306.4'85'082–dc21 CIP

Published in the United States by Cleis Press Inc.,
P.O. Box 14684,
San Francisco, California 94114.
Printed in the United States.

Cover & page design: Bernie Schimbke

Logo art: Juana Alicia
First Edition.
10 9 8 7 6 5 4 3 2 1

For Emma

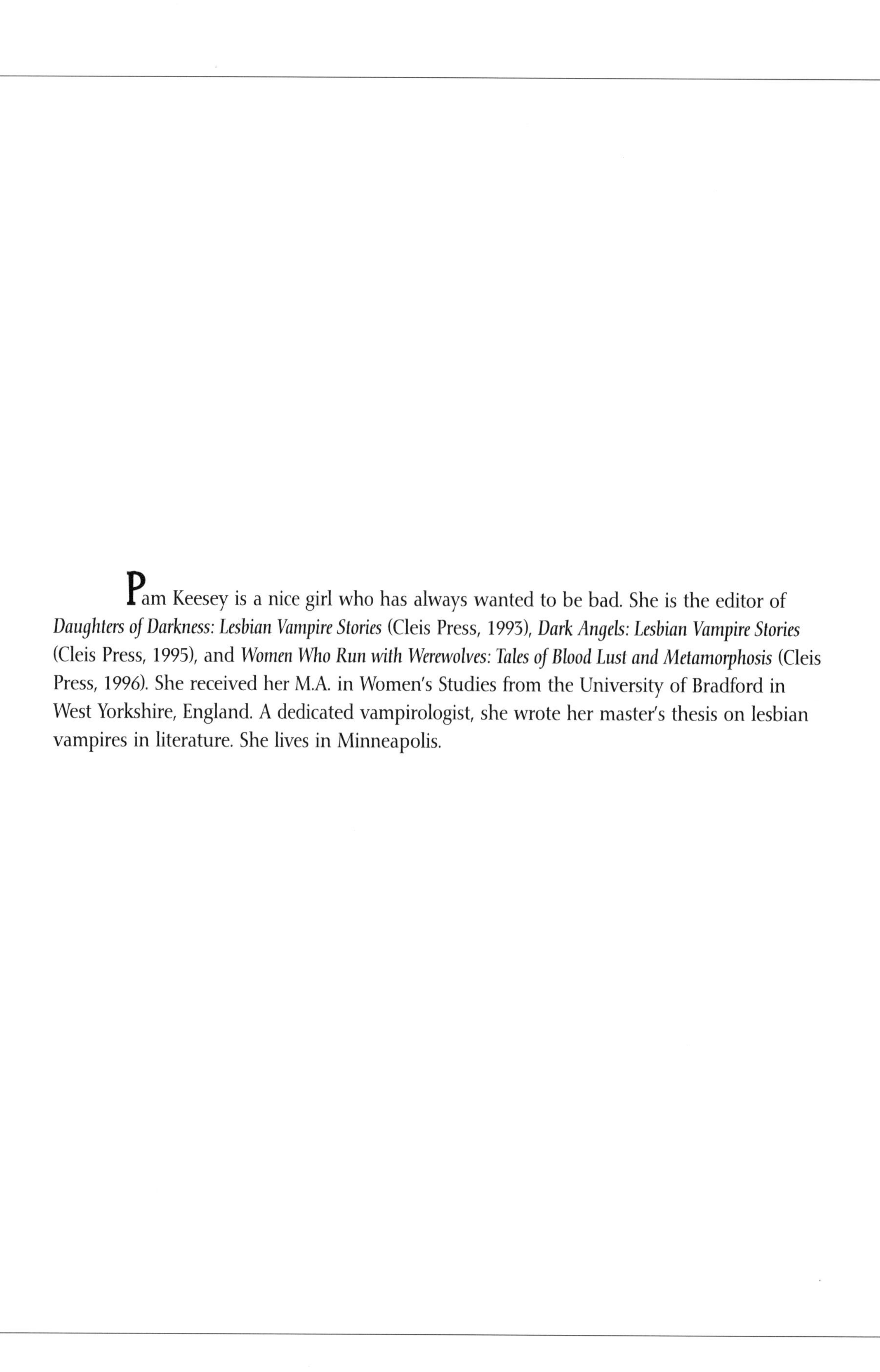

Pam Keesey is a nice girl who has always wanted to be bad. She is the editor of *Daughters of Darkness: Lesbian Vampire Stories* (Cleis Press, 1993), *Dark Angels: Lesbian Vampire Stories* (Cleis Press, 1995), and *Women Who Run with Werewolves: Tales of Blood Lust and Metamorphosis* (Cleis Press, 1996). She received her M.A. in Women's Studies from the University of Bradford in West Yorkshire, England. A dedicated vampirologist, she wrote her master's thesis on lesbian vampires in literature. She lives in Minneapolis.

# Table of Contents

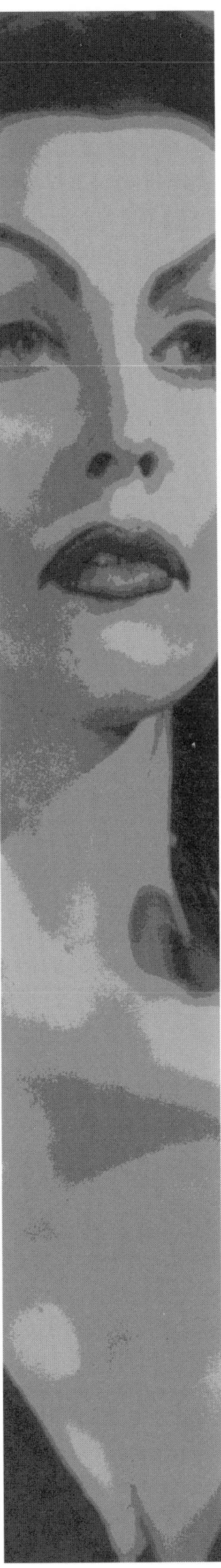

# Acknowledgments

**VAMPS** has truly been a collaborative effort and simply would not have been possible without the hard work and support of the Cleis Press team. Felice Newman's incredible writing and editing skills and her talent for reading my mind were crucial. Somehow she always knew what it was I was trying to say. This book would not exist without her. Many thanks, also, to Frédérique Delacoste, Bernie Schimbke, and Ned Takahashi. This book would be a mere shadow of its current self without their hard work and creativity. Their artistic vision and design talents are what really makes *Vamps* come alive. And thanks to Don Weise for encouragement, enthusiasm and hard work above and beyond any call of duty.

Thank you to Forrest J Ackerman who not only provided many of the images in this book, but also fostered a deep love and an appreciation for horror, science fiction and fantasy films and their stars among generations of film enthusiasts. Forry Ackerman is, without a doubt, an American legend. Thank you to Nancy Blair, artist and sculptor, for her talents and the permission to use her work to illustrate the many faces and facets of the Goddess. (For more information about Nancy Blair's artwork and The Great Goddess Collection, contact Star River Productions, Inc., P.O. Box 510642, Melbourne Beach, Florida 32951, or telephone (407) 953-8202).

Thanks, too, to Ron and Margaret Borst, whose passion for film and whose personal collection both inspired and motivated me.

Thanks, also to: Michael Waltz for his sharing his photographs and his love of Theda Bara; to Claudia Goldstein of Art Resource; and to Harriet at the Delaware Art Museum. And thank you, too, to many friends, especially from Minneapolis, Chicago, Los Angeles, and San Francisco, for your support, friendship, and diversion through what turned out to be an extraordinarily difficult year. I could not have done it without each and every one of you. Bless you all.

# Good Girls and Bad:

I don't know if I can tell you what first drew me to the femme fatale. It must have started at the tender age of four with my burgeoning love of horror movies, a passion that quickly developed into a love of all movies. Perhaps it was the first time I saw *The Wicked Lady* (1945). Or maybe it was simply that I was raised to be a good girl, obedient, polite, and friendly, always giving more than I took and asking little in return. And I was a good girl. My parents knew I would behave. My teachers thought me the ideal student. But in my mind's eye, and in the privacy of my own playtime, I lived the life of a lady pirate. Sometimes I was a dance hall floozie. I dearly wanted to be Cleopatra, floating down the Nile. But most of all, I wanted to be exciting, exotic, demanding. I wanted to be in control. And perhaps that's why I was so drawn to the dark and mysterious heroines of the movies I loved so much. They may have paid dearly for their freedom, but still, they lived life on their own terms.

As I got older, I realized that I wasn't the only one who wanted to break free from my Good Girl past. That's what the women's movement of the seventies was all about. By challenging the stereotypes of good woman and bad, Madonna and whore, feminists expanded the range of possibilities for girls like me. But what they didn't count on was how much girls like me loved the Bad Girl. We embraced her, not because she was everything we wanted to be, but because she let us express parts of ourselves that we had been taught to deny. And she looked so damn good doing it, too.

The femme fatale is a complex icon. She is, we are often told, what young women should never aspire to be, a cautionary example of the consequences of bad behavior. Men have used her as a representation of their fears and desires, marking themselves as innocent victims of her ill will. But there was a time when she was worshipped, too, in the form of the Devouring Mother, the destroyer aspect of the great goddess.

## Unless there is death, there cannot be life.

– Joseph Campbell, *The Power of Myth*

Although the phrase "femme fatale" is relatively new, the archetype she represents is as old as the ancient Goddess in whom she finds her roots. The Goddess was the ultimate expression of women's ancient power held in awe. Hers was and is a sexual power. She contained all of the mysteries of the universe within her; in her three phases, as girl, mother, and crone, she embodied the universal cycles of birth, death, and rebirth. (Contemporary Goddess worship is about reclaiming the power of the feminine, celebrating the cycle of women's lives and their fertility, and holding women's sexuality to be sacred.) With the transition to a god-centered religion and an emphasis on the male as the sacred center of the universe, the image of the Goddess was shattered. But even in god-centered religions, aspects of the Goddess were maintained. As the virgin, the mother, and the wife, she was celebrated and revered. In her dark element, the devouring mother who delivers her children unto death, we find the witch, the hag, and the whore. Her sexuality in service to the male gods was valued and revered, while her autonomous sexuality was viewed as corrupt and evil. From her status as the Mother of All Being, she was reduced to her various elements, a menagerie of monsters, demons and bogeys.

In the Middle Ages, the mystical and wondrous Other of the Goddess became the feared and dangerous witch, the woman who cast her spells and worked her magic to seduce both women and men into the realm of evil through desire. The rites and rituals associated with the Goddess were maintained throughout rural Europe with the help of village midwives and healers, the priestesses of their communities. They posed a direct challenge to the authority of the Church and its ability to maintain control over the religious expression of rural populations. To discredit these women and the religions they practiced, Church authorities proclaimed them witches, threats to good and decent people everywhere. The power of witches, like the power of the Goddess, lay in the sexual realm, for through "the wantonness of the flesh [witches] have much power over men." This aversion to women's sexuality fueled the hatred and fear of the witch hunts. In the hands of the Church, and with the help of the legal establishment, the once-sacred Goddess became the consort of the Devil, a danger and a threat to society and Christian faith. Worshipping her became a crime punishable by death.

The early eighteenth century, the "golden age of vampires," introduced the vampire as we now know it. Austrian authorities began systematic investigations into reports of vampirism. Drawing on folklore, legend, and the anxieties of people living in a plague-ridden era, the image of the vampire coalesced into the revenant, the creature who returns from the grave to drink the blood of loved ones. These tales, combined with earlier legends of ruthless leaders and blood-sucking ghosts, served as the foundation of the vampire literature that would begin to flourish in the nineteenth century.

**...communion is, above all, a penetrating of death, the great mother, because only death—which is night, sickness, and Christianity, but also the erotic embrace, the banquet at which the "stone becomes flesh"—will give us access to health, to life and to the sun.**

– Octavio Paz, *The Bow and the Lyre*

The femme fatale returned to command mainstream attention in the nineteenth century. Artists, writers, and designers drew on earlier images, the names and faces of the Goddess, the trickery and malevolence of witches, and the effusive imagery of the Romantics to create the femme fatale as we know her today. These artists came of age in the midst of a cultural revolution marked by the rise of industrialization and the formation of a European middle class. Women asserted their rights as the battle for women's suffrage came to the center stage. In the midst of it all was the spread of sexually-transmitted diseases, with syphilis at the forefront, that reached epidemic proportions by the end of the century. The femme fatale, deadly as ever, found a spotlight in the works of artists such as Dante Gabrielle Rossetti, Edward Burne-Jones, and Edward Munch.

Ever vigilant and always aware of her next opportunity, the femme fatale transformed, entering the twentieth century through the movies, a new medium and a burgeoning art form. The pristine prudishness of Victorian mores had made the evil woman a worthy foil. The sensationalism of the fallen woman was made socially acceptable by its implicit condemnation of her evil nature. The self-righteous tone of the message failed to dim the spectacular nature of the woman who left a trail of destruction in her wake.

As the techniques and styles of movie-making evolved, so did the image of the femme fatale. From the mortal woman whose capacity for evil warranted her reputation as "The Vampire," she became increasingly human, more sympathetic, and less deadly. She continued to be desirable, although she was still touched with the potential for danger. To love her was to come to a tragic end. She knew this and resisted the urge to draw her prey, but to love until death was her raison d'être, whether the death be hers or her lovers'.

As the culture surrounding sex and sexuality became more open, so did the representation of sexual women. By the 1950s, with World War II behind and *Playboy* just ahead, social norms and sexual politics made the femme fatale less threatening and more acceptable. The femme fatale was no longer fatal, at least not to others. Stripped of her power, but maintaining her allure, the femme fatale became the sex kitten. Her openness and her vulnerability marked her as women's sexuality tamed. By the 1960s, with the sexual revolution just around the corner, the sexual image of women in popular culture had returned once again to the supernatural for the edge, the frisson, the risk that we associate with the classic femme fatale. She is, after all, the woman who both attracts and repels. Once the now-diluted image of the vamp has become cliché, no longer able to instill fear, to repel, to incite passion, "The Vampire" returns to the silver screen, ready to work her charms.

In the nineties, vampires and vamps exist side-by-side. Mainstream films such as Francis Ford Coppola's *Bram Stoker's Dracula* and Neil Jordan's *Interview with the Vampire* have kept vampires in the forefront, while the vamp can be seen in a wide variety of movies, including *Basic Instinct*, *The Last Seduction*, *Bound*, and even *Irma Vep*.

The Dark Goddess is still with us. She is the vital essence of women's power—the power of life and death, the realm of darkness that leads us into the light. The once sacred image of the Devouring Mother has become profane, but she still exists and is still worshipped in her various forms and with her many names—Theda Bara, Louise Brooks, Greta Garbo, Marilyn Monroe, Sharon Stone. She tells us as much about who we are as individuals and a society as she does about herself, her needs, and her desires. *Vamps* traces the image of the fatal woman, both sacred and profane, to bring together the common threads and related themes that are the source of her power and a testimony to her endurance.

Pam Keesey
August 1997

Maila Nurmi as Vampira in *Plan 9 from Outer Space* (1956).

# 1

# "Good Evening. I Am... Vampira."

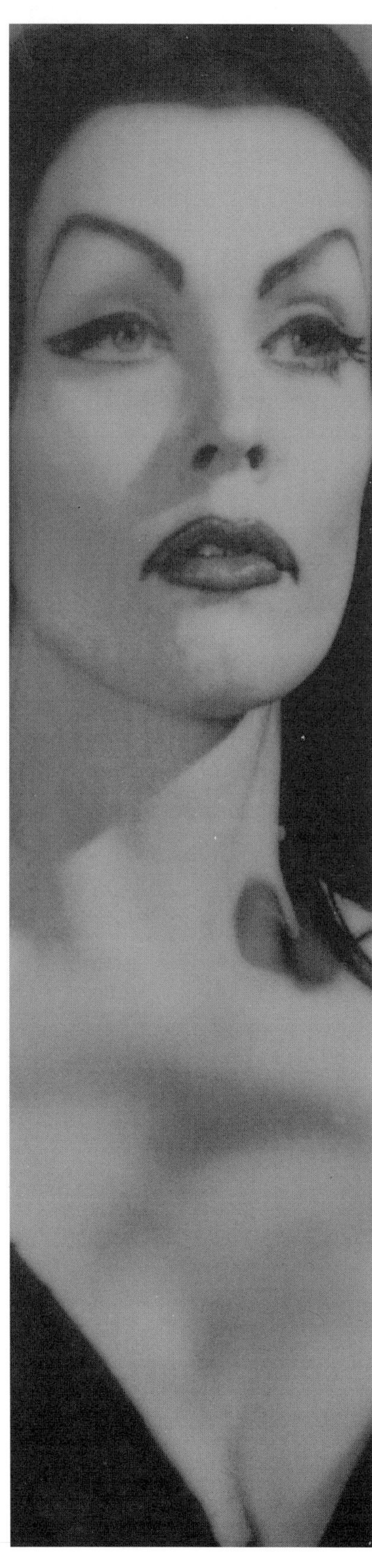

## Recipe for Vampira

2 oz. Theda Bara (vamp, vamp)

2 oz. Morticia (morbid Victoriana)

3 oz. Norma Desmond (Sunset Boulevard)

4 oz. Tallulah Bankhead (the voice, dahling)

2 oz. Marilyn Monroe (demons are a ghoul's best friend)

3 oz. Katharine Hepburn (Victorian English)

2 oz. Bette Davis (mama, baby)

3 oz. Billie Burke (dilettante insouciance)

3 oz. Marlene Dietrich (singing voice)

8 oz. *Bizarre* pin-up

—Maila Nurmi, in "The Vampira Chronicles" *Cult Movies*, no. 11

The scene is black and white, the setting gothic—a cathedral perhaps, or maybe a crypt. The lights are low; a candelabra is burning in the shadows. A low mist rises over the vast expanse of the foyer. A figure forms in the mist, advancing through a doorway at the far side of the room. She has an impossibly small waist, a wasp-like cinching between the swelling breasts and the voluptuous hips of a fertility goddess. Her black dress is in tatters, a form-fitting, cleavage-revealing shroud. Fingernails like straight razors extend from her long, pale fingertips. Her face is white, placid, with dark lips and kohled eyes. Eyebrows like flying arches frame her face, marking the space between her eyes and her black serpentine hair. Her gaze is fixed on the camera before her as she approaches, her eyes locked with yours. She raises her talons to her hair and screams an ear-piercing wail, a banshee's cry. In a voice deep and rich, a timbre reaching from beyond the grave, she speaks:

Theda Bara in *Cleopatra* (1917).

Carolyn Jones as Morticia in *The Addams Family* which made its television broadcast debut in 1964.

## "Good evening," she says. "I am...Vampira."

Vampira was the original horror movie hostess. She invited her viewers to watch old horror films such as *White Zombie* and *Fog Island*. In between reels, Vampira would share her vision of a hospital ward for would-be suicides called The Yellow Cross, or perhaps give the recipe for a foaming cocktail that "will absolutely kill you."

Vampira was the creation of actress and former Broadway chorus girl Maila Nurmi. With a piece of black fabric, fingernail scissors, and a wig, Nurmi created a costume inspired by the Charles Addams cartoon character Morticia. She debuted her costume at a Halloween Ball, where she hoped to get the attention of Charles Addams with the idea for a television series based on his *New Yorker* drawings. Although the Addams family did eventually become the basis for a television show in 1964, the role of Morticia Addams went to Carolyn Jones. That night, however, Nurmi drew the attention of Hunt Stromberg, Jr., program director at KABC

Gloria Swanson as Norma Desmond in *Sunset Boulevard* (1950).

## "I give epitaphs, not autographs."

– Vampira

Beginning in 1954, *The Vampira Show* was broadcast live. No kinescopes were ever made of the broadcasts, so there are no tapes of Vampira in action. Nurmi describes Vampira and her antics as "everything I repressed during my Depression childhood." Sex, macabre wit, and excellent comic timing all contributed to her pop icon status. To promote the show, she drove around L.A. in a chauffeured Packard, shaded from the sun by her black umbrella. She offered passers-by her trademark ear-splitting cry at stoplights. Among her interludes between movie reels were candlelight searches for her fictitious pet spider, Rollo, and baths in her cauldron of boiling oil. Despite her popularity, *The Vampira Show* was canceled only eight months after the show first aired. In 1956, Nurmi, broke and with few options, agreed to portray Vampira in Ed

television in Los Angeles. Stromberg suggested that Nurmi introduce his late-night horror line-up, without infringing on the Addams character. Nurmi played with the character, altering the costume, the makeup, and the overall effect. Drawing from classic Hollywood images and then-popular fetish magazines such as *Bizarre*, Nurmi created a unique character who melded images of sex and death. Unlike the Addams Family character whose straight, flapper-girl figure and bare feet exuded none of the exaggerated eroticism or the outright sexuality of Nurmi's character, Vampira was a Victorian vampire; a souped-up ghoul whose movie-star hair and makeup, hourglass figure, slit skirt, mesh hose, and platform shoes blended the sex-goddess fetishism of sex magazines, the dark side of the horror and gothic genres, and a *Grand Guignol* sense of humor. A welcome antidote to the idyllic world of television comedies and romantic dramas, Vampira became a local legend.

Tallulah Bankhead

Wood's now colossal cult movie, *Plan 9 from Outer Space*. In exchange for two hundred dollars and Wood's promise that she would not have a speaking role, Nurmi donned her Vampira costume and walked zombie-like, with arms outstretched, through Wood's tottering graveyard set. With fifteen minutes of footage, Wood constructed her role as the vampire's wife, a corpse reanimated by aliens with a mission to conquer the world. It was a role that Nurmi describes as "professional suicide." And the film might have been just another forgotten poverty-row production except for the posthumous "Golden Turkey" award given to Wood by the Medved brothers in 1981. With its revival as a cult favorite—a movie so bad that it's good—Nurmi has found an unexpected resurgence of popularity and a new generation of fans.

Maila Nurmi was born in 1921 in Lapland, Finland. Her parents emigrated to the United States when she was a baby. She describes her childhood as humble, growing up in a Finnish immigrant community in the Northwest during the depression, living among people she called "the poorest of the poor." "Movies were my escape as a child," she said. At age seventeen, she sought her fortune in New York, where among other roles she was cast in the Mae West musical *Catherine Was Great*. It was during a Broadway performance that she was discovered by Hollywood producer/director Howard Hawks. "I was to be the 'new' Lauren Bacall," Nurmi recalled, "but I wasn't his cup of tea, nor was he mine, so we went our separate ways."

Marilyn Monroe sang "Diamonds Are a Girl's Best Friend" in *Gentlemen Prefer Blondes* (1953).

**"Vampira never changes, any more than Mickey Mouse does."**

– Maila Nurmi

When asked about her early influences, Nurmi mentions the Dragon Lady from Milton Caniff's Sunday comic strip "Terry and the Pirates." She also describes a film in which she saw a woman who was "strong, powerful, independent, beautiful, and rich. She was everything I wanted to be. The movie was *Snow White*, and that's when I fell in love with the Evil Queen." Vampira is a character much like her Disney counterparts, whether *Snow White's* Evil Queen, *Sleeping Beauty's* Maleficent, or *101 Dalmatians'* Cruella DeVil. She embodies the archetypal images of sex and death, both exaggerated and sensationalized to the point of caricature. Nonetheless, the archetype she represents is as old as time. She is the dark goddess, the devouring mother. She is the vamp and the femme fatale. She is beautiful, alluring, and sensuous, yet she is also dangerous if you come too close. Women, especially outspoken women who assert themselves to lay claim to their desires, have been identified with demons, witches, and vampires throughout history. The belief that woman is the root of all evil is commonly held, and many world religions still revolve around this basic "truth." This belief in the essential wickedness of woman has informed images of women not only in religion, but also in art, music, literature and in film. Wicked women have permeated popular culture at every level. That these women—bold, assertive, sexual, and autonomous—have been equated with vampires speaks volumes to societal expectations of women's behavior.

Katharine Hepburn

## "What horror story isn't about sex?"

– Jack Sullivan, *The Penguin Encyclopedia of Horror and the Supernatural.*

The classic vampire may be the aristocratic older gentleman, whose genteel and otherworldly accent haunts the highways and byways—and, if you are not careful, the parlors and bedrooms—of everyday life. But the vampire tradition is far older than Bram Stoker's *Dracula*, or even Polidori's *The Vampyre*. The vampire appears in stories of ancient goddess worship, a tradition that was used to fuel the witch craze as much as it has inspired films such as *Basic Instinct*.

Vampires are typically depicted as reanimated male corpses who drink the blood of the living in order to maintain their "undead" state. Yet the earliest vampires were women. From the early image of the devouring goddess, the mother who ate her children, came tales of birth demons, the spirits of women who died in childbirth and preyed upon pregnant women and children in grief and rage: the *cihuapipiltin* of Aztec Mexico, the *langsuyar* of Malaysia, the *pontianak* of Indonesia. These birth demons were also known to linger at crossroads, ready to attack wayward young men. Such bogeys became a part of a storytelling tradition in which foreign women of mystery and allure would seduce young men, leading them to their ultimate demise. From these tales evolved our modern vampire, the romantic figure who first courts, then seduces, and finally kills its prey.

It is the seductive quality of the vampire that has made it one of the most popular of all of the classic monsters. The vampire's attack, the drawing of blood, often resembles an embrace, a kiss, an intimate exchange between two lovers. Bela Lugosi and Christopher Lee, the two men most famous for their portrayals of Count Dracula, drew heavily on the erotic image of the vampire to develop their characters. Furthermore, the animal nature of sexuality is an underlying theme throughout Bram Stoker's novel. The threat Count Dracula poses to "polite" society is embodied by his animalistic desires and his pursuit of "good" women. Yet bad women are also integral to the story of Count Dracula. The most eroticized passage in the book is Jonathan Harker's first encounter with the three vampire women residing in Dracula's castle:

Bette Davis

> I was not alone.... In the moonlight opposite me were three young women.... They came close to me and looked at me for some time.... All three had brilliant white teeth that shone like pearls against the ruby of their voluptuous lips. There was something about them that made me uneasy, some longing and at the same time some deadly fear. I felt in my heart a wicked, burning desire that they would kiss me with those red lips....
>
> ...I lay quiet, looking out under my eyelashes in an agony of delightful anticipation. The fair girl advanced and bent over me till I could feel the movement of her breath upon me. Sweet it was in one sense, honey-sweet, and sent the same tingling through the nerves as her voice, but with a bitter underlying the sweet, a bitter offensiveness as one smells in blood.
>
> ...There was a deliberate voluptuousness which was both thrilling and repulsive, and as she arched her neck she actually licked her lips like an animal, till I could see in the moonlight the moisture shining on the scarlet lips and on the red tongue as it lapped the sharp white teeth.... I closed my eyes in a languorous ecstasy and waited–waited with beating heart.

**"Horror immobilizes us because it is made of contradictory feelings: fear and seduction, repulsion and attraction. Horror is a fascination... Horror is immobility, the great yawn of empty space, the womb and the hole in the earth, the universal Mother and the great garbage heap.... With horror we cannot have recourse to flight or combat; there remains only adoration or exorcism."**

– Octavio Paz, *Hieroglyphs of Desire*

Harker knows that he is in a dangerous situation. He already suspects that Dracula is something other than human. He realizes he is imprisoned within the walls of Castle Dracula and forbidden to enter any locked room. It is behind one of these locked doors that Jonathan finds the vampire women awaiting his arrival. His journal entries reveal that he is terrified. At the same time, he finds the women so enticing and their attentions so arousing that he can't resist their allure. He can only close his eyes and wait.

The "brides" of Dracula—like the women of Goethe's "Bride of Corinth," Keats' "Belle Dame Sans Merci," LeFanu's "Carmilla" and the other female vampires that came before and after them—use sexuality to lure their unwary prey. They close in on their victims with promises of untold pleasures and delights, when suddenly they strike like the snakes in an idyllic garden. Their true nature is revealed as they sink their fangs into soft flesh.

Billie Burke, most famous for her role as Glinda the Good Witch in *The Wizard of Oz* (1939).

Marlene Dietrich in *A Foreign Affair* (1948). (Photo courtesy of Forrest J Ackerman).

The twin themes of sex and death permeate all of Stoker's work, and many people have made speculations about Stoker's own most intimate desires based on the undercurrent of sexual repression that defines his work. But Stoker certainly wasn't the first to combine these themes or to apply them to vampire literature. Sex and death—and the mythology, fear, and anxiety that surround these subjects—are the very basis of vampire tales and legends. These twin themes also form the foundation for myths and stereotypes about women, sexuality, and childbirth. This image of woman as death comes to the fore in the discussion of the femme fatale, literally the fatal woman. Women's sexuality has been so demonized that for a woman to be sexually demanding or even sexually autonomous is to enter the realm of the supernatural. The folklore of the sexually-insatiable man—the Don Juan or the Lothario—describes a romantic hero, an enviable and admired individual. The sexually-insatiable woman, on the other hand, is the witch, the vampire, the predatory woman whose victims are the women and men she seduces.

**"...it is the unexpected, what is dissonant and even unpalatable in a woman that makes her a heroine worth bothering about."**

– Margo Jefferson, *The New York Times,* Dec. 10, 1996

Cover from John Willie's *Bizarre,* a fetish magazine published from 1948 to 1959.

The femme fatale and the female vampire are more than sisters in crime. They are mirror images, each borrowing qualities from the other until they are nearly identical. The femme fatale acquires the supernatural qualities of the vampire, while the female vampire, not as physically strong as her male counterparts, relies on her ability to lure her prey with promises of sexual pleasure. If she is neither mature enough nor sophisticated enough to use sexuality as her lure, she is reduced to preying on children. Whether flesh and bone or from beyond the grave, women who have stepped outside the realm of socially approved behavior so upset the status quo that they are labeled monstrous. Like the bloodthirsty goddess who dances on the body of her dead lover, or Sharon Stone's ice-pick wielding bitch goddess, these women come from a long, proud, and tragic history.

As deadly as the femme fatale is, the danger she poses isn't always one of aggression. The femme fatale is sometimes passive, as the lure of her beauty and sensuality alone are enough to bring men to their ruin. Helen is said to have brought the fall of Troy through her incomparable beauty. Eve, on the other hand, is a figure rife with contradictions. Passively created from Adam's rib, she is the aggressor when it comes to the "forbidden fruit." Created by God as Adam's companion, she is revered as the mother of all of human-kind. As the temptress seduced by the serpent, who then seduces Adam, she is both sexually desirable and infinitely dangerous. It is

Maila Nurmi revived her Vampira costume to portray the vampire's wife in Ed Wood's *Plan 9 from Outer Space* (1956).

Eve, after all, who causes man's exile from Paradise. The femme fatale is often a paradox, embodying contradictory qualities—aggression and passivity, desire and repulsion, purity and filth, innocence and guilt. She is at once sacred and profane. She may also be both insatiable and frigid, motherly and wanton, savior and destroyer. In her landmark work, *The Second Sex*, Simone de Beauvoir describes woman as "Other." Woman is the *tabula rasa* on which all things that are "not man" are written. As the Other, a projection of all things that man both fears and adores, woman becomes all of the qualities that are assigned to her, no matter how dichotomous or contradictory the images may be. "The myth of woman as infinite Other," she writes, "also entails its opposite."

The construction of the fatal woman as the Other is based on desire and fear. She has been both worshipped and loathed throughout history. It is this representation of women that serves as the basis for our current mythology about women and sexuality. It is in the Goddess as Devouring Mother that we find the earliest blood-drinkers, the women who seduce both women and men into the labyrinth of desire, eroticism, and even death.

The femme fatale is a measure of social change and cultural anxiety. Her incarnations as the witch, the vampire and the vamp are as much a commentary on history as a representation of the enduring archetypes of sexual women. When she is not at the forefront of cultural expression, she hovers just beneath the surface, awaiting the opportunity to reveal herself once again.

**"The woman who makes free use of her attractiveness—adventuress, vamp, femme fatale—remains a disquieting type. The image of Circe survives in the bad woman of the Hollywood films. Women have been burnt as witches simply because they were beautiful. And in the prudish umbrage of provincial virtue before women of dissolute life, an ancient fear is kept alive."**

– Simone de Beauvoir, *The Second Sex*

Gloria Swanson as Norma Desmond in *Sunset Boulevard* (1950).

2

# The Goddess in Every Vampire

In the beginning there was the Goddess, Creator of the universe, the Mother of All Being. She was not the center of the universe, but the universe itself, and all early worship centered around her figure. In the beginning, the Goddess reigned alone. She brought forth not only the first people, but also heaven and earth, from deep within her own being.

Early images of the Goddess were of a single cosmic parent who contained her male element within her. At some point, she acquired a male consort. In some myths, she gave birth to a son who then became her mate, while in others, she gave birth to twins who went on to populate the earth with their children. The Goddess' young lover was the personification of nature, his life and death representing the changing of the seasons. It was the Goddess who was responsible for his resuscitation and recovery, on which the renewal of the seasons depended.

The Egyptian Goddess Nut as an arched figure touching the "ends of the earth" with her fingers and toes. (Photo courtesy Nancy Blair, Star River Productions. Copyright 1995.)

"The Goddess is a lovely, slender woman with a hooked nose, deathly pale face, lips red as rowan berries, startlingly blue eyes and long fair hair; she will suddenly transform herself into sow, mare, bitch, vixen, she-ass, weasel, serpent, owl, she-wolf, tigress, mermaid or loathsome hag. Her names and titles are innumerable."

– Robert Graves, *The White Goddess*

The Goddess as the Mother of All Being was revered in her three aspects: as young woman, as matron, and as crone. She was the birth-giver, mother, and death-bringer all in one. She was Parvati-Durga-Uma in India, Hebe-Hera-Hecate in Greece, Ana-Babd-Macha (the Morrigan) in Ireland. It is in her three aspects that we find the roots of the modern Christian trinity of the Father-Son-Holy Spirit.

**"The Night Mare is one of the cruelest aspects of the White Goddess. Her nests, when one comes across them in dreams, lodged in rock-clefts or the branches of enormous hollow yews, are built of carefully chosen twigs, lined with white horse-hair and the plumage of prophetic birds and littered with the jaw-bones and entrails of poets. The prophet Job said of her: 'She dwelleth and abideth upon the rock. Her young ones also suck up blood.' "**

– Robert Graves, *The White Goddess*

The Goddess of the trinity, or the Triple Goddess, embodied more than her features; she also embodied her domain. She was the Goddess of the Sky, the Earth, and the Underworld. As Goddess of the Underworld, the Dark Goddess, she was concerned with birth, procreation, and death. As the Goddess of Earth, she was concerned with the seasons, spring, summer and winter. As Goddess of the Sky, she represented the Moon and her three phases: the new moon, full moon, and waning moon. The Goddess personified each of these domains in three phases. As the New Moon, as Spring, as Birth, she was the Maiden; as the Full Moon, Summer, and Mother she was the Matron; as the Old Moon, Winter, and Death she was the Crone. The Goddess, the Lady of the Beasts, could take any form at will. She could be both virgin and aged, mother and child. As the Lady of the Beasts, she could also take the form of animals. Most commonly she was associated with snakes, cats, and birds. Many ancient texts refer to the Goddess of a Thousand Names, and, conversely, the thousand goddesses who were aspects of the one Goddess who is the Mother of All Life.

The Goddess Trinity—Maiden, Mother, Crone. (Photo courtesy of Nancy Blair, Star River Productions. Copyright 1995.)

The myths and legends that explain the origins of life were told and retold, each story changing bit by bit with the retelling of the tale. Stories changed as people settled, moved, and resettled. Travelers took with them beliefs and practices from one place and transported them to another. The beginning of the end of Goddess worship is tied to the rise of God-centered cultures such as the Apollonians who revered the Sun-God. The Goddess, no longer considered the supreme deity, was reduced to a secondary role which complemented and supported the role of the God. Her many entities were broken down, and her many aspects became discrete and concrete individuals. Robert Graves, in *The White Goddess*, describes the stories and tales that displaced the image of the supreme Goddess, stories that cast her in a different, arbitrary, and often hostile light. For example, in the heroic epics of Hercules and Odysseus, men go forth to do battle with beasts, many of whom are female—the Sirens, the Gorgon, Calypso. The hero conquers the beast, usurping her strength and her authority. Both the monster and the maiden who is rescued (Penelope, for example) are emanations of the Goddess. By splitting the Goddess in two, the hero can save one aspect of the Goddess while destroying another. It is a pattern that is repeated throughout history, from the ancient epics to classic fairy tales as retold by Walt Disney

Medusa Gorgon, the serpent-goddess representing female wisdom, was also the Destroyer aspect of the goddess Athene. "A female face surrounded by serpent-hair was an ancient, widely recognized symbol of divine female wisdom, and equally of the 'wise blood' that supposedly gave women their divine powers." — Barbara Walker, *The Woman's Encyclopedia of Myths and Secrets*. (Photo courtesy of Nancy Blair, Star River Productions. Copyright 1994.)

The creation of individual characters from the many aspects of the universal Goddess diminished her and further weakened her role. The Goddess of Art, Music, and Poetry was incorporated into the image of the muse, with first three muses, and later nine, assuming the inspirational role for creative acts that were once the domain of the Goddess alone. The Goddess of the Underworld, with her many names, faces, and animal familiars, became numerous birth demons, night mares, succubi, and hags.

"I, the natural mother of all life, the mistress of the elements, the first child of time, the supreme divinity, the queen of those in hell, the first among those in heaven, the uniform manifestation of all the gods and goddesses—I who govern by my nod the crests of light in the sky, the purifying wafts of the ocean, and the lamentable silences of hell—I whose single godhead is venerated all over the earth under manifold forms, varying rites, and changing names... call me by my true name, Queen Isis."

– Apuleius, *The Golden Ass*

Lilith with bird feet and her familiar, the screech owl. In the Middle Ages, owls were thought to be witches in bird form. As "night-hags," the Daughters of Lilith were believed to creep into the beds of sleeping men. "[T]hey were presumed so expert at love-making that after an experience with a Night-Hag, a man could never again be satisfied with the love of a mortal woman." — Barbara Walker, *The Woman's Encyclopedia of Myths and Secrets.* (Photo courtesy of Nancy Blair, Star River Productions. Copyright 1987.)

*The Golden Ass*, also known as *Metamorphoses*, tells the story of Lucius, a devotee of the Goddess Isis. It contains what is considered to be the first recorded vampire story. It is also widely believed to be the first written novel. Written in the second century A.D., its author was an acolyte of the Temple of Isis, and it is Isis in the end who assists the main character in completing his metamorphosis. Lucius is a traveler who, by his own folly, is transformed into an ass. Through these adventures, he collects stories and tales which form the basis of the novel. In one tale, the hero meets Aristomenes who tells a story of his friend, Socrates, having been seduced by a witch named Meroe. Having escaped her clutches, Socrates has found a temporary refuge and is asleep in an inn, sharing a room with Aristomenes. Aristomenes is still awake when the door is suddenly ripped from its hinges. It is the witch, Meroe, and her sister, Panthia. For Socrates' betrayal of Meroe, she and Panthia slit his throat, draining his blood into a wine sack and ripping out his heart. In the original Latin, these women are called *lamiae*. In translation, the word *lamiae* appears variously as witch, vampire, hag, or sorceress. Further on in the novel, there is another vampire-like woman named Pamphile who is a shape-shifter. She takes the form of an owl, a nocturnal creature associated with wisdom, the underworld, and particularly with the Jewish demon Lilith whose familiar is the screech owl.

Demeter, the mother phase of the trinity Kore-Demeter-Persephone, whose rites included overt sexuality in pursuit of regeneration and forgiveness of sins. (Photo courtesy Nancy Blair, Star River Productions. Copyright 1987.)

**"The power of witches is more apparent in serpents, as it is said, than in other animals, because it is through the means of a serpent the devil tempted woman."**

– *Malleus Maleficarum*

It is in the image of the devouring mother/monster that it is easiest to see the Goddess as vampire. The Hindu goddess Kali, like Meroe or Panthia, is a bloodthirsty goddess, the dark aspect of the universal Mother Goddess Devi. Kali is said to have fangs or tusks, four arms, claws wielding swords and spears, and a necklace of severed heads. In one tale, Kali joins the goddess Durga to fight the demon Raktabija, whom she defeats by drinking all of his blood. Kali is also a prominent deity within the tradition of Tantric Hinduism as Creator, Protector, and Destroyer. In Tantra, the way of salvation is through the sensual delights of this world. Kali represents these often forbidden pleasures and teaches that life relies on death, and that in confronting death there is liberation.

This image of Kali hints at the sacred roots of sexuality found in goddess religions. In goddess religions, sex was a

Cretan Snake Goddess. "Immortality was the special province of the skin-shedding Serpent and the blood-bestowing Goddess from earliest times." — Barbara Walker, *The Woman's Encyclopedia of Myths and Secrets*. (Photo courtesy of Nancy Blair, Star River Productions. Copyright 1990.)

holy offering to the Creator, a celebration of the source of life. To celebrate the Goddess with sexual rites was to carry on a legacy of worship. As the role of the Goddess was challenged and usurped, the rites and rituals attributed to her were either assimilated and incorporated into God—centered worship or completely vilified. The sexual rites that were part and parcel of women's autonomy came to be regarded as lustful, shameful, and disgraceful. Sex outside of procreation was classified as evil. Among the sins of the demonized goddess and her demon children is the propensity for sex.

According to the Talmud, Lilith was the first wife of Adam. Made not of his rib, but equal in creation, Lilith refused to be subservient to Adam. Rather than concede to his authority, Lilith escaped to the Red Sea, the dwelling place of demons. There she lived in a cave, consorted with demons, and gave birth to thousands of demon children. God sent three angels—Senoy, Sansenoy and Semangeloff—after Lilith to command her to return to Adam. She refused, even after the angels threatened to kill one hundred of her children every day. In retaliation, Lilith swore vengeance on newborn infants, saying that she could be stopped from snatching the souls of babes only if confronted by an amulet bearing the names of the three angels.

Lilith slipped into the beds of men, seducing them in their sleep, causing sinful dreams and nocturnal emissions, while also impregnating herself with even more demon children. Her children, the *lilim*, were demons who, like their mother, seduced men in their sleep, drank the blood of the living, and killed newborn children.

With dark hair and eyes and luminescent skin, Lilith was said to be very beautiful. She could change herself into any form she wished, human or animal, and could appear as an old woman or as a young and beautiful maid. She stole life energy from children in the form of their souls and from men in the form of their "seed" or "life essence." She seduced young women to lust and vanity. In one tale, a young woman who has been possessed by Lilith is cursed by her father to flit from man to man in the form of a bat.

**"The Dark Devi [Kali Ma] is the embodiment of the powers of women which have been so long suppressed, denigrated, or denied by patriarchy-our spirituality, our sexuality, our fertility, our anger, and our inherent freedom."**

– *The Divine Mosaic*

Lilith was a night goddess related to the Babylonian Lilitu, a dark goddess whose realm included the underworld, birth, sexuality and death. According to the Kabbalists, Lilith was a harlot, an impure woman who, jealous of Eve, took the form of a serpent in order to seduce Eve. The Zohar, a sacred Jewish text, warns repeatedly that men must be ever vigilant against Lilith:

> … behold that hard shell, the embodiment of evil, Lilith is always present in the bed-linen of man and wife when they copulate, in order to take hold of the sparks of the drops of semen which are lost—because it is impossible to perform the marital act without such a loss of sparks—

That Lilith was present even in the purest of marital intentions implicates all associations with women as potentially evil. That Lilith also had the power to seduce Eve bears witness to the fact that all women contain within them the potential to betray their assigned role.

Lamia and her demon namesakes, the *lamiai*, too, are relics of the dark goddess. The *lamiai* also held the powers of transformation, appearing as beautiful young women in order to attract and seduce men. In her goddess form she was Lamia, the Serpent-goddess, the serpent being symbolic of the wisdom and of the third aspect of the Triple Goddess, the Crone. In mythology, she was the Queen of Libya and the lover of the Greek god Zeus. His wife Hera, in a jealous rage, killed all of Lamia's children. Lamia, in her grief and anger, became a demon who killed children by devouring them or by sucking their blood. Like Lilith in the Talmud's garden of Eden, the *lamiae* are described as coarse-looking, with the lower bodies of serpents, and the ability to mesmerize their victims by making themselves appear young and beautiful.

Wanda Ventham as a blood-sucking moth that seduces its prey in the guise of a beautiful woman in *The Vampire Beast Craves Blood* (1969). (Photo courtesy of Forrest J Ackerman.)

The Goddess Empusa also has been closely identified with the demons. Her namesakes were the empusae who, like the *lamiae* and *lilim*, were demonic creatures who took the form of beautiful women in order to seduce men, lure them away from their wives and children, and bring about their ruin. Empusae are said to enter the bodies of their prey in order to eat the flesh and drink their blood.

Lilith, Lamia, and Empusa are all related to a plethora of spirits called "birth demons," the souls of women who either have died in childbirth or have given birth to stillborn children. In Malaysia she was called the *langsuyar*; in Indonesia she was the *pontianak*; the Aztec referred to her as *cihuapipiltin*; and the Greek named her *strige*. More modern images of these blood-sucking birth demons can still be found in *la Llorona* of Mexico and the American southwest, the banshee of Ireland, and the White Lady of Europe. In their grief and rage, they are said to prey on the children of mortal women and their mothers. Like the Dark Goddess, who as death-bringer devours her own children, these demon women are cast as the enemies of the innocent, namely children.

**"against every instinct of human or animal nature, [witches] are in the habit of eating and devouring the children of their own species."**

– *Malleus Maleficarum*

According to Robert Graves, it is precisely because the Dark Goddess holds power over life and death that it is necessary to understand and appreciate her gifts and to pay homage to her as the source of all poetry. Even in modern times, far removed from the ancient worship of the goddess or an understanding

The "brides" of Dracula standing over the body of Renfield in *Dracula* (1931). (Photo courtesy of Forrest J Ackerman.)

of the sacred sources of poetry, Graves argues that the power of the goddess is found in the works of truly great poets. He names Sappho as one poet who understood the power of the Goddess. Shakespeare, he writes, "knew and feared her" noting the presence of the Triple Goddess in *Macbeth* as the three "wyrd sisters" who preside over the cauldron, telling of Macbeth's fate and inspiring Lady Macbeth to kill Duncan. He also sees the Goddess in Shakespeare's "magnificent and wanton" Cleopatra and the "damned witch Sycorax" in *The Tempest*. He also refers to John Keats, whose poem "La Belle Dame Sans Merci" is about a woman who brings death and leaves it in the form of the "lily on his brow," and Keats' poem "Lamia," which celebrates the deadly power of the ancient Serpent-goddess in a modern guise.

Perhaps, too, lesser poets understand the power of the Goddess. Bram Stoker, author of not only *Dracula*, but also *The Lair of the White Worm* and *The Woman of the Shroud*, was certainly familiar with the legends and folktales of the ancient Goddess. In *The Lair of the White Worm*, Lady Arabella March is cold and cunning, an acolyte of the ancient serpent who lives in the cavern at the center of her estate. *The Woman of the Shroud* is a veiled woman in the image of the Crone, the mysterious creature found at and returned to the sea. *Dracula*, of course, is the story of a male monster, a threat to polite society and good women. But is it a coincidence that in the bowels of Castle Dracula there are three women who await their prey with a heightened sensuality, a deathly kiss, a cold embrace? These women, often referred to as the brides of Dracula, have popularized the idea of a harem-like arrangement in which a single male vampire is surrounded by a bevy of beautiful vampire women. They are never referred to as "brides" in the novel, but as "young women," "weird sisters," and "ghostly women." At the end of the story, when Abraham Van Helsing enters the castle to kill the women, he refers to them simply as "sisters." Like the "wyrd sisters" who are the witches of Shakespeare's *Macbeth*, perhaps Stoker's "weird sisters" are remnants of Dark Goddess, the Triple Hecate.

**"The reason why the hairs stand on end, the eyes water, the throat is constricted, the skin crawls and a shiver runs down the spine when one writes or reads a true poem is that a true poem is necessarily an invocation of the White Goddess, or Muse, the Mother of All Living, the ancient power of fright and lust-the female spider or the queen-bee whose embrace is death."**

**– Robert Graves, *The White Goddess***

In Greece, Hecate was the patron goddess of midwives and healers. She is sometimes referred to as Herodias and became known as the Queen of Witches during the Middle Ages. The many references to the names of goddess, to moon rituals and sex rites, and the vilification of midwives in the *Malleus Maleficarum* make the links between the goddess worship that continued in the rural areas of Europe and the Church's desire to quell these practices. The characteristics that the authors of the *Malleus Maleficarum* associated with evil women—powerful, dangerous, sexual, and a threat to children and young women—essentially provided the blueprint for the image of the femme fatale.

Joan Crawford.

# 3

# "All Wickedness Is But Little to the Wickedness of a Woman."

Amanda Donahoe as Lady March in *Lair of the White Worm* (1988). "We must answer the question why God permits witchcraft to affect the generative powers more than any other human function....For it is on account of the shamefulness of that act, and because the original sin due to the guilt of our first parents is inherited by means of that act. It is symbolized...by the serpent, who was the first instrument of the devil." — *Malleus Maleficarum*. (Photo courtesy of Forrest J Ackerman.)

In 1984, President Reagan mandated the creation of a national commission on pornography. Two years later, the Commission, headed by Attorney General Edwin Meese, published its 1,960-page, two-volume final report. The report outlined the specific dangers of pornography and its effect on women, children, and families. To determine these dangers, the Commission made specific efforts to acquire as much of the offensive material as they could gather. Testimony was heard from anonymous "victims of pornography." A vice-squad detective took the Commission on a slide-show "tour" of an adult bookstore, complete with "peep show" booths. An FBI agent presented a slide show on the "evolution of pornography." The Commission immersed itself in "obscene" material in order to become "experts" on the "evils" of pornography.

**"What else is a woman but a foe to friendship, an inescapable punishment, a necessary evil, a natural temptation, a desirable calamity, a delectable detriment, an evil of nature, painted with fair colors!"**

– *Malleus Maleficarum*

Five hundred years earlier, another commission of so-called experts, with the blessing of the Pope, took it upon themselves to investigate the dangers of witchcraft. The perpetrators of evil, they found, were not pornographers but women who "entice men away from [good], and...betray them into evil." Their report, the *Malleus Maleficarum*, outlines the specific sexual feats of women whose powers could tempt men, lure them from the path of righteousness, and hinder the legitimate act of procreation between a husband and wife. The authors' obsession with the sexual prowess of these witches is illustrated by what, at the time, must have been considered lurid tales of illicit sexual activity. The power of witches to incite lust, cause frigidity, obstruct conception, and obscure the "male organ" so that it "appears to be entirely removed and separate from the body," are so thoroughly detailed one can't help but assume that the authors were as obsessed with sex as any member of the Meese Commission. One would think these devout men fantasized as much about women's sexual exploits as any director of a seventies lesbian vampire film or a movie patron screening *Basic Instinct*.

**"When the member is in no way stirred, and can never perform the act of coition, this is a sign of frigidity of nature; but when it is stirred and becomes erect, but yet cannot perform, it is a sign of witchcraft."**

– *Malleus Maleficarum*

The *Malleus Maleficarum*, also known as the *Hammer of Witches*, has been called the "most important and the most sinister work on demonology ever written." First published in 1486, the *Malleus* served as the handbook for witch-hunts that soon followed as well as the inspiration for all subsequent treatises dealing with witchcraft. The authors, Heinrich Kramer and James Sprenger, both Dominican priests residing in Germany, took to heart the Biblical command: "Thou shall not suffer a witch to live." The *Malleus Maleficarum*, with incredibly detailed descriptions of the specific elements of witchcraft, became the standard by which women's ability to do evil was measured.

Sharon Stone in a reptilian pose complete with scale-like sequins.

Kramer and Sprenger's text benefitted by Gutenberg's development of moveable type and of the printing press thirty years earlier, which made books more widely available than ever before. The *Malleus Maleficarum* was accessible to all clergy of the day and was consistently reprinted throughout the years following its first publication. Sprenger and Kramer set in print a variety of anti-woman beliefs drawn from the Bible and from misrepresentations of rural religious practices based on goddess worship and the work of healers and midwives. Their work helped to shape the myths, legends, and folktales of "dangerous" women for generations to come.

"...three general vices appear to have special dominion over wicked women, namely, infidelity, ambition, and lust...since of these three vices the last chiefly predominates, women being insatiable, etc., it follows that those among ambitious women are more deeply infected who are more hot to satisfy their filthy lusts..."

– *Malleus Maleficarum*

Witches brewing up a hailstorm. From the title page of Ulrich Molitor's *De lanijs et phitonicis mulierbus*, Colonge, 1489.

In 1484 Pope Innocent VIII made a statement concerning the pressing need to recognize the public dangers of witchcraft and to address rising opposition to the witch-hunts that had begun to take place. In his statement, a papal bull, Pope Innocent recognized that "many people of both sexes" are witches who:

> unmindful of their own salvation and straying from the Catholic Faith, have abandoned themselves to devils, incubi and succubi, and by their incantations, spells, conjurations, and other accursed charms and crafts, enormities and horrid offences, have slain infants yet in the mother's womb, as also the offspring of cattle, have blasted the produce of the earth, the grapes of the vine, the fruits of trees, nay, men and women, beasts of burthen, herd-beasts, as well as animals of other kinds, vineyards, orchards, meadows, pastureland, corn, wheat, and all other cereals; these wretches furthermore afflict and torment men and women, beasts of burthen, herd-beasts, as well as animals of other kinds, with terrible and piteous pains and sore diseases, both internal and external; they hinder men from performing the sexual act and women from conceiving, whence husbands cannot know their wives nor wives receive their husbands; over and above this, they blasphemously renounce that Faith which is theirs by the Sacrament of Baptism, and at the instigation of the Enemy of Mankind they do not shrink from committing and perpetrating the foulest abominations and filthiest excesses to the deadly peril of their own souls, whereby they outrage the Divine Majesty and are a cause of scandal and danger to very many.

Elisabeth Brooks as the nymphomaniac werewolf woman in *The Howling* (1981). "There is incidentally a question concerning wolves, which sometimes snatch men and children out of their houses and eat them, and run about with such astuteness that by no skill or strength can they be hurt or captured. It is to be said that this sometimes has a natural cause, but is sometimes due to a glamour, when it is affected by witches." — *Malleus Maleficarum*. (Photo courtesy of Forrest J Ackerman.)

## "All witchcraft comes from carnal lust which in women is insatiable."

– *Malleus Maleficarum*

The particular incidents Pope Innocent describes are called *maleficia*, the misfortunes, injuries, and mishaps for which no immediate explanation can be found. *Maleficia* were attributed to the vindictiveness of witches. The crime of witchcraft included not only specific *maleficium*, but also involved four specific requirements as outlined in the *Malleus*: the renunciation of the Catholic faith; some form of devotion to or pact with the devil; the offering of unbaptized children to Satan; and carnal intercourse with incubi and succubi. Because of the renunciation of the Church witchcraft is heresy, and the authors of the *Malleus* are very clear throughout

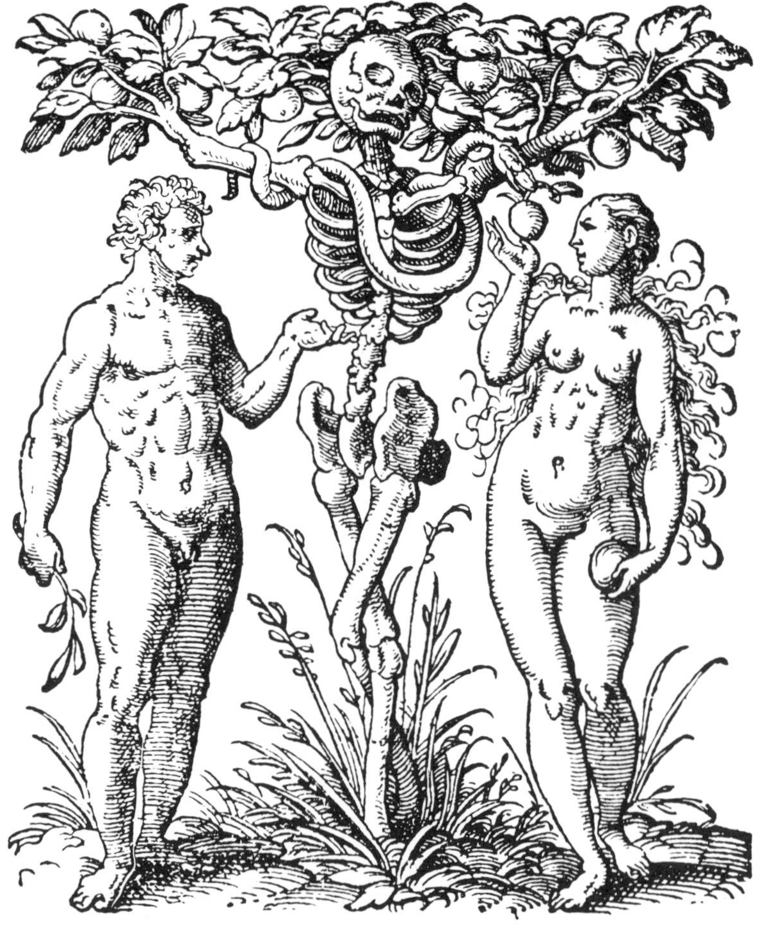

Adam and Eve with the Tree of Knowledge as Death. Woodcut by Jost Amman, from Jacob Ruegg's *De conceptu et generatione hominis*, Frankfurt, 1587.

their work that women are the primary source of such heresy. "There are three things in nature," they write, "the tongue, an Ecclesiastic, and a Woman, which know no moderation in goodness or vice...since they are feebler both in mind and body, it is not surprising that they should come more under the spell of witchcraft." They concede that male witches, whom they call wizards, do exist, but the authors also point out that the heresy of witchcraft takes its name from the more powerful of the two practitioners of the art. "Blessed be the Highest Who has so far preserved the male sex from so great a crime: for since He was willing to be born and to suffer for us, therefore He has granted men this privilege."

**"Witches are so called on account of the blackness of their guilt... they distract the minds of men, driving them to madness, insane hatred, and inordinate lusts."**

– *Malleus Maleficarum*

The *Malleus* is divided into three parts. The first part addresses the threat witchcraft poses to society and the pressing need for officials, as well as the public to recognize its dangers. Parts two and three detail what witches are capable of doing, how to counteract these evil deeds, and advice on how to bring these women to trial, secure a conviction, and pass a sentence.

The threat that evil women pose to society is often reduced to their ability to seduce young women into their evil ways. The *Malleus Maleficarum* describes how witches, in an effort to serve the devil, "entice innocent girls to swell the numbers of their perfidious company." The authors of the *Malleus* warn that while witches may use spells and blights to drive honest women to their cause, their method for enticing the young is decidedly different: "toward young girls, more given to bodily lusts and pleasures, they observe a different method, working through their carnal desires and the pleasures of the flesh."

The sexual nature of the crimes witches commit is a recurring theme throughout the work. Among the questions addressed by Kramer and Sprenger are: "Whether Witches can Sway the Minds of Men to Love or Hatred; Whether Witches can Hebetate the Power of Generation or Obstruct the Venereal Act; and, Whether Witches may work some Prestidigitatory Illusion so that the Male Organ appears to be entirely removed and separate from the Body." Sex plays such an important role in deeds of witchcraft because, "God allows them [witches] more power over this act, by which the first sin was disseminated, than over other human actions." Eve, too, is implicated in this classification of witches. She is the first temptress, the woman responsible for the loss of paradise:

Two vampire women fight over the body of a dead child in *Return of Count Yorga* (1971). (Photo courtesy Forrest J Ackerman.)

> For though the devil tempted Eve to sin, yet Eve seduced Adam. And as the sin of Eve would not have brought death to our soul and body unless the sin had afterwards passed on to Adam, to which he was tempted by Eve, not by the devil, therefore she is more bitter than death.

As all women are the daughters of Eve, so all women are prone to lead men into temptation. Since the days of Creation, women have used their wiles to affect the course of human history. With their ability to control men through licentiousness, women have brought down great civilizations:

> ...nearly all the kingdoms of the world have been overthrown by women. Troy, which was a prosperous kingdom, was, for the rape of one woman, Helen, destroyed, and many thousands of Greeks slain. The kingdom of the Jews suffered much misfortune and destruction through the accursed Jezebel, and her daughter Athaliah, queen of Judah, who caused her son's sons to be killed, that on their death she might reign herself; yet each of them was slain. The kingdom of the Romans endured much evil through Cleopatra, Queen of Egypt, that worst of women. And so with others. Therefore it is no wonder if the world now suffers through the malice of women.

Witch giving a ritual kiss to Satan. From R.P. Guaccius' *Compendium Maleficarum*, Milan, 1626.

"Certain witches, against the instinct of human nature, and indeed against the nature of all beasts, with the possible exception of wolves, are in the habit of devouring and eating infant children."

– *Malleus Maleficarum*

Midwives were a particular target of the *Malleus*, for "[n]o one does more harm to the Catholic Faith than midwives." Harm done to the Church as a result of the "horrible crimes" committed by midwives includes: preventing couples from performing "the carnal act" or otherwise preventing a woman from conceiving; causing the abortion or miscarriage of an unborn child; and finally, eating children or offering children as sacrifices to the devil. All of these acts diminish the numbers of Catholic believers by preventing the survival of children who would otherwise be born into the faith.

The *Malleus* is rife with animosity toward midwives. The authors believed that "midwives…surpass all others in wickedness" and cause "the greatest injuries to the Faith." As an example, they cite the case of a woman who confessed to killing more than forty children by "sticking a needle through the crowns of their heads into their brains, as they came out of the womb." If the midwife didn't kill the child outright, she baptized the child in the name of the devil. "As soon as the child is born, the midwife, if the mother herself is not a witch, carries it out of the room on the pretext of warming it, raises it up, and offers it to the Prince of Devils…"

Midwives at that time not only delivered babies. They were also healers, counselors and pharmacists. They possessed knowledge of cures and herbal medicines handed down from generation to generation, and many scholars have suggested that their methods for passing on knowledge were linked to rural pagan practices. References are made to the witches who "ride with Diana" or their ties to Herodias, another name for the goddess Hecate. These practices, including women coming together in ritual celebration, the blessing of a newborn child by the light of the moon, or the sharing of charms and amulets to affect a certain outcome of events, are all noted in the *Malleus Maleficarum* and are identified as proof of the evil and fiendish ways of midwives. Their greatest crime, according to Kramer and Sprenger, was their ability to postpone the second coming of Christ through the killing of children:

The vampire wrapped in a shroud rises from her grave in *Vampire Lovers* (1970). (Photo courtesy Forrest J Ackerman.)

Natassia Kinski in *Cat People* (1982). Along with the owl, bat, and the wolf, the animal most commonly associated with witches is the cat. In *Cat People,* a young woman fears that sexual arousal will turn her into a blood-thirsty animal. (Photo courtesy Forrest J Ackerman.)

> by this means the Last Judgement is delayed, when the devils will be condemned to eternal torture; since the number of the elect is more slowly completed, on the fulfillment of which the world will be consumed. And also, as has already been shown, witches are taught by the devil to confect from the limbs of such children an unguent which is very useful for their spells.

Many theories for this hatred of and prejudice toward midwives have been suggested, including jealousy on the part of priests whose roles in the parish were challenged by the preference villagers showed for the local women healers. Others have suggested that the embryonic medical profession felt the need to wipe out this woman-controlled arena of folk medicine. Whatever the combination of forces that contributed to the fear of witches, midwives and healers, the fact that they were hated, mistrusted and maligned by certain members of the Church is without question.

Vampires are never specifically mentioned in the *Malleus*. Although there were many reports of vampire-like incidents, the word vampire didn't enter the popular lexicon until the early eighteenth century following an epidemic of reported vampire attacks in Eastern Europe. Even so, there are anecdotes about specific cases of witchcraft that have more than a passing similarity to reports of vampires. In one instance they describe the case of a man who, having discovered his child missing from its cradle late at night, swore that he had seen a "congress of women" kill his child, drink its blood and devour it.

**"[The] feminist agenda is not about equal rights for women. It is about a socialist, anti-family political movement that encourages women to leave their husbands, kill their children, practice witchcraft, destroy capitalism and become lesbians."**

**– Pat Robertson, in a fundraising letter in support of the Iowa Committee to Stop ERA**

In another tale, a town was almost completely depopulated by the death of its residents. There was a rumor that a deceased woman was gradually eating her burial shroud, and that the plague would not end until the entire shroud had been eaten. The grave was opened, and the body was found with half the shroud ingested through the mouth. The woman's head was cut off and removed from the grave, and, it was said, the plague ceased at once. When an inquisition was held, it was found that she had been a witch in life and that the sins of the old woman had been visited upon the people of the town since her death.

Blood-sucking, shroud-eating and plague-like epidemics are associated with both vampires and witches, so much so that blood-sucking witches and vampires have become nearly synonymous. In Victor Hugo's *Notre Dame de Paris*, Esmeralda, a gypsy, is accused of having "taken part in the agapes, sabbath, and malefices of hell, with larvae, masks, and vampires...." Esmeralda is found guilty of witchcraft and the murder of an officer, and she is sentenced to death, "a sentence by virtue of which this vampire [ista stryga], together with her goat...be executed."

Esmeralda's little goat, Djali, is also tried for witchcraft. As Esmeralda's familiar, the goat is an accomplice to murder and receives the same sentence, to be "hanged and strangled on the town gibbet." The goat was also required to pay a fine of "of gold in reparation for the crimes... of witchcraft, magic, lechery, and murder."

George Cole as Count Harthog avenging his sister's death by killing the vampire in the opening sequence of *Vampire Lovers* (1970). "...witches must not be punished like other Heretics with lifelong imprisonment, but must suffer the extreme penalty....the penalty for them is the confiscation of their goods and decapitation." —*Malleus Maleficarum*. (Photo courtesy Forrest J Ackerman.)

"I use my eyes to invite you,
My lips to delight you
And you never can tell when I'll use my
Teeth to bite you.
They say that I'm a witch
And that I weave a spell...."

– Eartha Kitt, *I'd Rather Be Burnt as a Witch*

The affinity of witches to animals is a common theme, and one that is repeated throughout the *Malleus*. Witches were said to ride to the Sabbat on "certain beasts" and were likely to "cohabit with beasts." Snakes, cats, wolves and owls are among the animals most favored by witches and, in earlier times, animals that also had strong associations with images of the goddess. Witches not only consorted with animals but were likely to take their form as well, employing the same sorcery they used to appear as beautiful young women or haggard old crones. The power of the bestial woman, and the sexual and animalistic implications that the image implies, became a popular theme in art in the late nineteenth century in the works of artists such as Dante Gabrielle Rossetti, Edward Burne-Jones, and Edward Munch.

Elvira.

4

# The Rise of the Modern Vampire

"This is the story of the Countess who bathed in the blood of girls.... For the last two hundred years Csejthe Castle has lain in ruins on its rocky spur of the Lesser Carpathians.... But the ghost and the vampires remain, and so does the earthenware pot which used to contain the blood which was about to be poured over the shoulders of the Countess; that is still there in a corner of the cellars."

– Valentine Penrose, *The Bloody Countess*

The vampire rising from her grave in *The Vampire and the Ballerina* (1960). (Photo courtesy Forrest J Ackerman).

The bodies of three young women are discovered in the depths of Bathory's castle in *Countess Dracula* (1970). (Photo courtesy Forrest J Ackerman.)

taken to investigate the allegations. There were rumors, too, that the Countess bathed in the blood of her victims as a way of maintaining her youthful beauty. According to the legend, a servant girl was brushing Bathory's hair and accidentally yanked a snarl, pulling the Countess' hair. The Countess responded by turning around and smacking the girl across the face, causing her nose to bleed. The blood spurted from the girl's nose to Bathory's hand. When the Countess wiped the blood away, she swore her skin looked younger and healthier. From then on, she insisted in bathing in the blood of young women to retain her youth and beauty. Although there is no evidence that such bathing took place, trial records confirm that the Countess and her accomplices killed an extraordinary number of young women. The victims were tortured, often stripped naked, and most were bled. She was found guilty, her accomplices executed, and the Countess was imprisoned for life in her own castle. She died in 1615, never having shown remorse nor admitted guilt. Today, she lives on in a vast array of vampire films and literature.

Belief in vampires was further legitimized by the works of scholars like Dom Augustin Calmet, a French Roman Catholic biblical scholar whose interest in vampires was prompted by the waves of vampire reports in Eastern Europe and Germany in the seventeenth century. He collected as many of the accounts of vampires as he could find and then offered his commentary on the phenomenon. He noted that "it seems impossible not to subscribe to the belief which prevails in these countries that these apparitions do actually come forth from the graves and that they are able to produce the terrible effects which are so widely and so positively attributed to them." Published in 1746, his book, with the rather daunting title of *Dissertations sur les Apparitions des Anges des Démons et des Esprits, et sur les Revenants, et Vampires de Hongrie, de Bohème, de Moravie, et de Silésie,* became a bestseller, including three editions in French, one in German, and one in English. Calmet was criticized by his colleagues for taking vampires seriously, and his work was widely dismissed. However, he did preserve much of the vampire literature of the eighteenth century, making both the reports and the folklore available to a new generation of writers who would find inspiration in the tales of the undead.

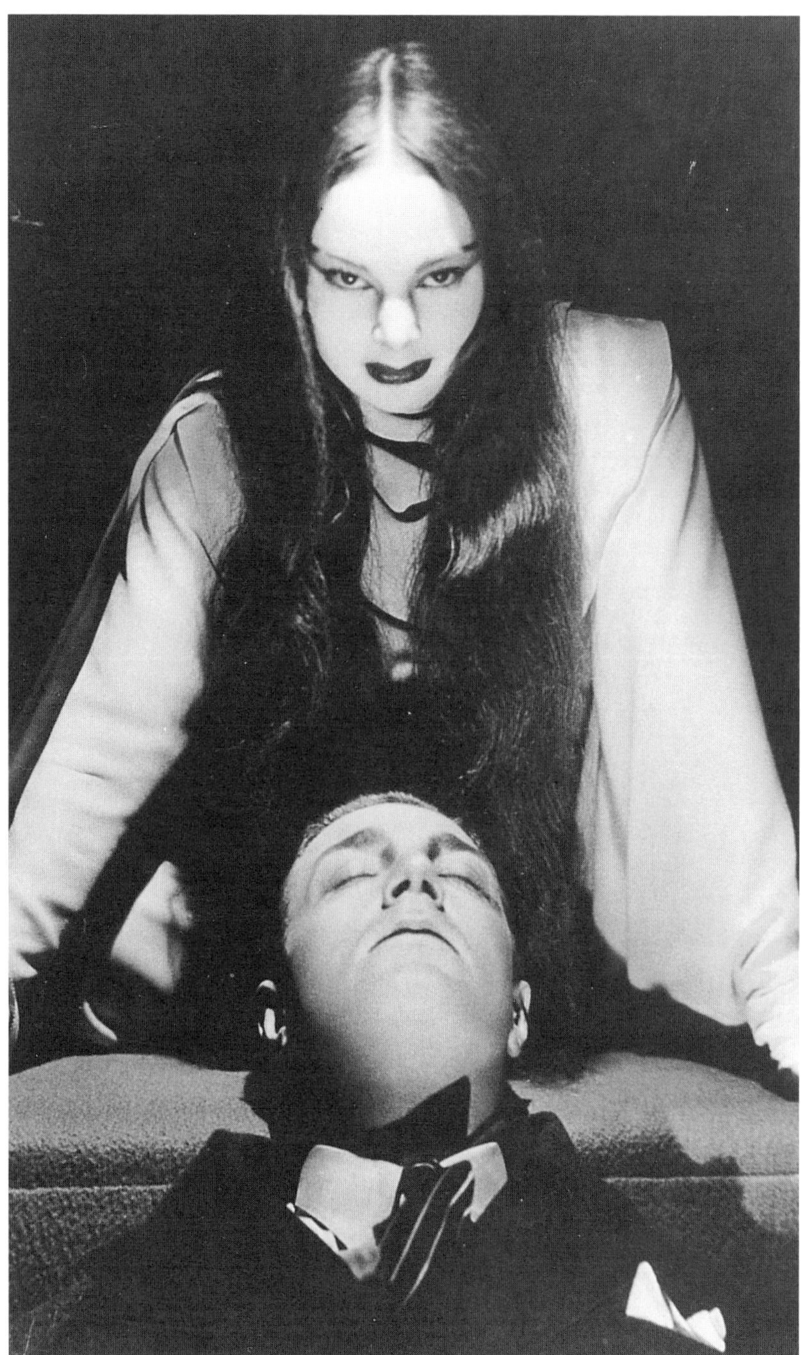

The vampire peers over the body of her victim in a publicity still from *Mark of the Vampire* (1935). (Photo courtesy Forrest J Ackerman.)

The earliest literary vampires were women. "The Bride of Corinth" by Johann Wolfgang von Goethe, was published in Germany in 1797. The poem was based on a Greek tale in which a young virgin named Philinnon returned from the dead to be with Machates, her mortal love. The first vampire tale written in the English language, "Christabel" by Samuel Taylor Coleridge, appeared at about the same time. Christabel first meets Geraldine, the vampire of the poem, in an abandoned forest under a full moon. She invites Geraldine to stay at her family's castle. Once she is in Christabel's bedroom, Geraldine undresses Christabel and then undresses herself. Christabel describes the sight of Geraldine's breasts as "one to dream of, not to tell." Geraldine approaches her, stirring a "desire with loathing strangely mix'd." She knows

Yet Geraldine nor speaks nor stirs;
Ah! What a stricken look was hers!
Deep from within she seems half-way
To life some weight with sick assay,
And eyes the maid and seeks delay;
Then suddenly, as one defied,
Collects herself in scorn and pride,
And lay down by the Maiden's side!–
And in her arms the maid she took,
Ah wel-a-day!
And with low voice and doeful look
These words did say:

"In the touch of this bosom there worketh
a spell,
Which is lord of thy utterance, Christabel!
Thou knowest to-night, and wilt know
tomorrow,
This mark of my shame, this seal of my sorrow;
But vainly thou warrest.
For this is alone in
Thy power to declare,
That in the dim forest
Thou heard'st a low moaning,
And found'st a bright lady, surpassingly fair;
And didst bring her home with thee in love
and in charity,
To shield her and shelter her from the damp air."

– Samuel Taylor Coleridge, "Christabel"

that touching Geraldine's "bosom" is somehow dangerous and forbidden, but it is a temptation she can't resist. Christabel awakens the next morning, ashamed of the events that took place during the night. Christabel is strangely weak and lethargic, while Geraldine is brighter, stronger, more refreshed. In the end, Geraldine abandons her.

Vampires were also the theme of John Keats' poem, "Lamia." Published in 1819, "Lamia" draws on a Greek biography by Philostratus entitled *Life of Apollonius of Tyrana* in which a young man becomes enamored of a woman who turns out to be one of the mythological lamia, a serpent-like woman who survives by sucking the blood of men and children. Although in the original tale as told by Philostratus, the lamia admits to "feeding upon young and beautiful bodies," the lamia of Keats' poem drains the young man's life energy in a form of psychic vampirism. In the same year, Keats also wrote "La Belle Dame sans Merci." In this poem, a young knight meets a lady with whom he becomes completely entranced. He visits her underground home and there sees "pale warriors," whom, he is told, he will soon join. Many critics have suggested that the "Belle Dame" of the poem is Death and the mark she leaves, "the lily on his brow," is tuberculosis, the disease that killed Keats' mother and eventually killed him.

One of the most famous and influential vampire stories ever written is "Carmilla," by Irish ghost story writer and journalist J. Sheridan LeFanu. "Carmilla" is a prose reworking of Coleridge's "Christabel," telling the tale of Millarca Karnstein, a mysterious young woman of aristocratic lineage with pale, luminous skin, dark hair, and serpentine features. Assuming the name Carmilla, she "befriends" Laura, the young heroine for whom she proclaims her love. Laura soon becomes ill, sapped of her strength and vitality by Carmilla's all-consuming love.

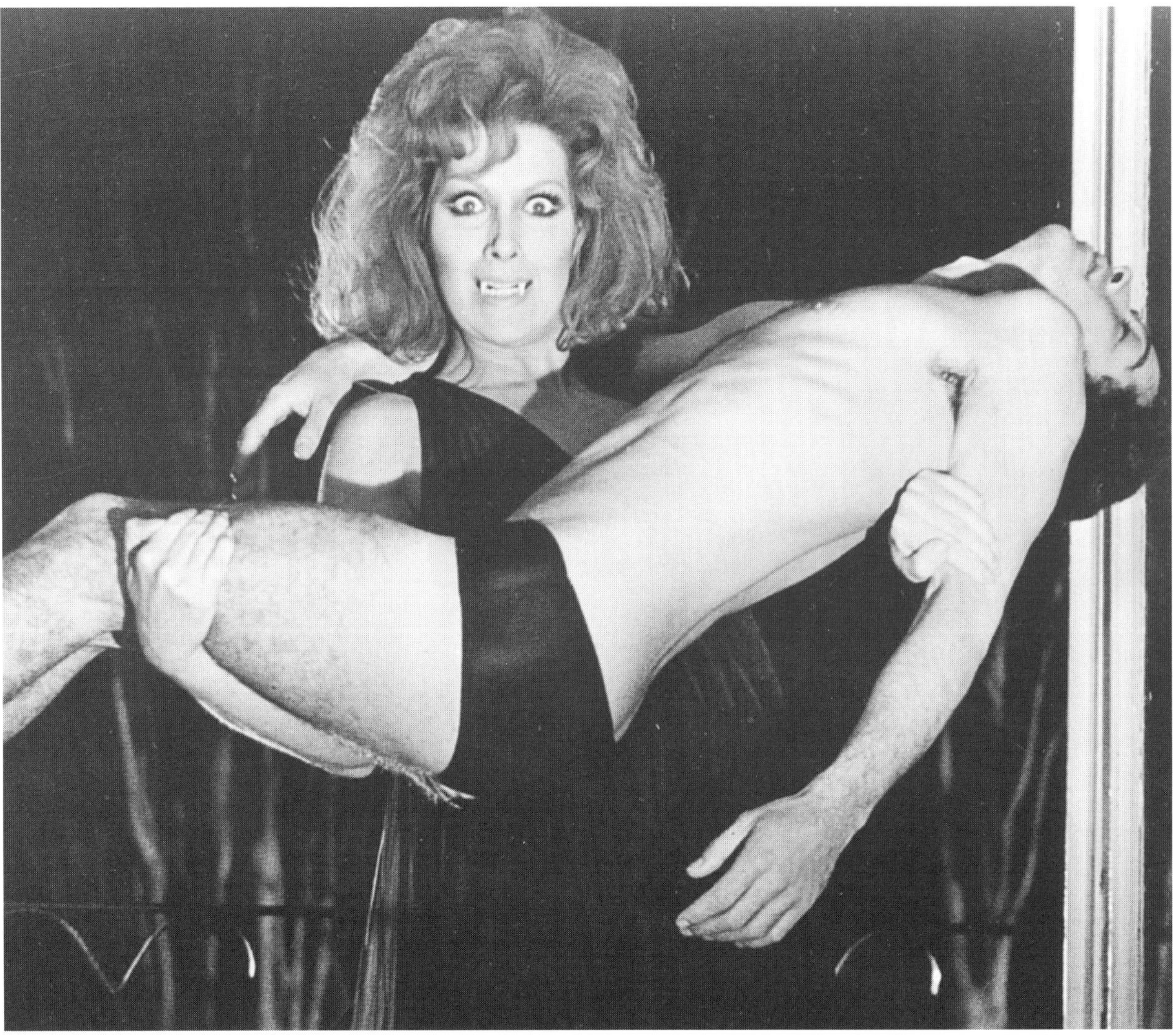

A vampire woman ready to feast on the blood of a man in *The Vampire's Night Orgy* (1972). (Photo courtesy Forrest J Ackerman.)

**"Carmilla is no more and no less than a very clever young woman determined to run off with the girl of her choice...."**

– Barbara Grier, writing as Gene Damon in *The Ladder* (1971), the magazine of the vanguard lesbian organization Daughters of Bilitis

Carmilla's vamping of Laura is a tale of seduction. In the novella, Laura describes her dreams in which "there came a sensation as if a hand was drawn softly along my cheek and neck. Sometimes it was as if warm lips kissed me, and longer and more lovingly as they reached my throat." The sexual nature of these dreams becomes even more apparent as the dream continues. Her breathing becomes heavy, and she begins a sob that brings a "sense of strangulation...turned into a dreadful convulsion," at which point Laura feels her senses leave her. When Carmilla enters Laura's room in physical form, she does so in the form of a cat which bites Laura, sucking blood from the veins in her breast.

Carmilla's serpentine features and her cat familiar link her to the witches of the *Malleus Maleficarum*, influencing the depiction of vampires to follow. The erotic nature of the story, particularly the overt sexuality and implied lesbianism of Carmilla herself has become a model for the representation of women as vampires.

Carmilla shares her aristocratic heritage with two other influential vampire tales of the eighteenth century. John Polidori, physician to the controversial Romantic poet Lord Byron, wrote a short story, "The Vampyre" (1819), in which the vampire is loosely based on Byron himself. Polidori was with Byron in Geneva, along with Percy Bysshe Shelley and Mary Godwin, on the evening in 1816 when bad weather prompted an evening of telling ghost stories—the same evening that Mary Godwin, who would soon marry Percy Shelley, began the tale that would become her novel, *Frankenstein*. Using a fragment of a tale started by Byron, Polidori wrote a story of two friends traveling in Greece. One of the friends, Lord Ruthven, dies. Before his death, he extracts a promise from his friend not to reveal anything about the conditions leading up to and including his death. His friend agrees and returns to England only to find that Ruthven is a vampire and has not only returned to England, but also claimed his sister as his next victim.

Annette Vadim as Carmilla in *Blood and Roses* (1961). (Photo courtesy of Forrest J Ackerman.)

Sir Francis Varney, the central character of the first vampire novel, *Varney the Vampire*, also has aristocratic ties. First published as a serial drama in the 1840s, Varney was, before becoming a vampire, a strong supporter of the British Crown during the Commonwealth and was killed by Cromwell's men for his support of the exiled King. Varney, as he comes to understand his vampiric nature, is revealed as a man of both honor and integrity, although his needs drive him to kill in his search for human blood.

Tragic beauty, whether in the form of men of honor who are driven to destroy those around them or women whose allure entraps the women and men who fall in love with them, is a recurring theme throughout the eighteenth century and well into the nineteenth. That death could be beautiful and evil could be desirable are sensibilities that define much of the work of the Romantic era. Evil could be as noble as good, and death more glorious than life.

**"With Milton, the Evil One definitely assumes an aspect of fallen beauty, of splendour shadowed by sadness and death; he is majestic though in ruin."**

– Mario Praz, *The Romantic Agony*

Ingrid Pitt as Carmilla dispatching the governess, Kate O'Mara in *Vampire Lovers* (1970). (Photo courtesy Forrest J Ackerman.)

The evil nature of the aristocracy and the aristocratic nature of evil captured the imagination of many writers throughout the ages. Milton's Satan in *Paradise Lost* is one early example of the proud and alluring anti-hero, imbued with all the grand characteristics of the angels of Heaven, yet brought into sinister focus as the Prince of Darkness. The sublime nature of the brooding anti-hero was often infused into eighteenth century literature and continued to influence writers well into the next century. The Byronic hero was the mortal counterpart to Milton's fallen angel. The femme fatale, too, was redefined by the idea of terrible beauty. In the mythology of the Middle Ages, beauty was a form of sorcery, a glamour thrown up by witches to make the horrid appear lovely. The femme fatale, by contrast, is beauty incarnate. Her appearance is no illusion. Still, to look such beauty in the eye is to risk death.

Carroll Borland as Luna in a publicity shot for *Mark of the Vampire* (1935).

# 5

# The Romantic Agony: 19th Century Images of the Fatal Woman

She is a beautiful woman. Her stance is erect, her image imposing. Her eyelids are lowered and her head is just slightly tilted back. Her long hair flows down around her shoulders. Her lips are beautifully sculpted, her gaze smoldering. There is a dangerous edge to her seductive allure, an eroticism just this side of animal lust. She is the femme fatale, the dark Venus, the demon Lilith, the irrepressible Eve.

*Astarte Syriaca* by Dante Gabriel Rossetti. Astarte was a Babylonian fertility goddess, "the bringer of death and decay...and who in the manner of certain insects destroyed her lovers." –Patrick Bade, *Femme Fatale*. (By permission of City Art Gallery of Manchester.)

**She is older than the rocks among which she sits; like the vampire she has been dead many times, and learned all the secrets of the grave.**

– Walter Pater, commenting on the Mona Lisa

Images of the femme fatale proliferated in the art and literature of the second half of the nineteenth century. Artists such as Dante Gabriel Rossetti, Edward Burne-Jones, and Edward Munch portrayed her on canvas, while writers such as Oscar Wilde and John Keats and musicians such as Georges Bizet featured her in poetry, plays, novels and operas. Eventually she appeared in arts and crafts, peering from necklaces, perched on ash trays and inkwells, and gazing up from soup bowls. She also became prominent in advertising campaigns, edging her way into the popular consciousness.

Although the image of the femme fatale is associated with the art and literature of the late nine teenth century, the phrase itself is more recent. The *Oxford English Dictionary* traces the use of the phrase in English to George Bernard Shaw in 1912. Regardless, the image of woman as portrayed through much of the last half of the nineteenth century is one that, even now, is understood as the quintessential fatal woman. She is the woman who, by means of her overwhelmingly seductive charms, leads men into danger, destruction, and even death.

Artists and writers of the nineteenth century drew from images of classical mythology, history, and literature for their work. From the Bible came Eve, Jezebel, Delilah, Judith and Salome. Eve, who like Pandora, brought evil and death to humankind, was often represented with large, writhing snakes, equating her not only with original sin but also overt sexuality. Judith, the Jewish widow who decapitated the Philistine general Holofernes after making love to him; Salome, who demanded the head of John the Baptist as reward for dancing before Herod; and Delilah, who destroyed Samson by cutting his hair, betrayed him to his enemies, and then put out his eyes—all found renewed popularity. Lilith, too, was a popular subject for writers and painters.

*The Shipwrecked Man and the Sea* by Arthur Rackham. (By permission of Victoria & Albert Museum, London/Art Resource, NY.)

Greek and Roman mythology offered Helen of Troy, Circe, Medusa, Medea and the Sirens. Circe, the witch from Homer's *Odyssey*, was able to transform men into swine. Medusa was remembered as the terrible Gorgon with hair of snakes whose hideous stare could turn men to stone. In ancient Greece, Medea was a moon goddess whose chariot was drawn by snakes. Her magic arts controlled the sun, moon and stars; she could restore the dead to life in her magic cauldron. Medea, wife of Jason, killed her children and her husband's lover in grief and rage at her husband's desertion. The Sirens held a distinctive place in the art of this era. The Sirens were the magic women of Cyrene in Homer's *Odyssey*, women who cast spells on ships and the men who sailed them, causing them to wreck on the rocky coast of Cyrene's shores. Sirens and their sisters—mermaids, nymphs, and other inhabitants of the sea—received particular attention because of the dangers of travel by sea. Drowning was a common fate, and death by drowning is a recurring theme in the art of the late nineteenth century. In Edward Burne-Jones' *The Depths of the Sea* (1887), the femme fatale as mermaid has her arms wrapped round a young man who is being pulled to the bottom of the ocean. *Circe Poisoning the Sea* (1892), a painting by John William Waterhouse, depicts the goddess endangering all whose livelihood depends on the sea.

Gloria Swanson, wearing furs in the tradition of the nineteenth century femme fatale. (Publicity photograph.)

Women's affinity to the natural world, especially to various beasts of prey, is another favorite subject in nineteenth century art. Images of women who were half human and half beast were common. The Sirens, mythological women whose upper torsos were attached to the bodies of birds, were painted as chickens, vultures and hawks. Lilith and Lamia made appearances as women with the bodies of snakes. Mermaids, of course, were half fish, half human. Other images emphasized the feline nature of women. The Sphinx, with her woman's head and leonine body, found a new audience in this genre.

Women's bestiality, if not represented literally in half-human form, was alluded to in a variety of ways. The femme fatale was often accompanied by animals, her companions an extension of her animal nature. Snakes slithered between her breasts or around her neck; lions and tigers rested at her feet, awaiting her command. She was seen lounging on a bed of tiger skins or elaborately clothed in furs.

Regardless of the source, inspiration, or historical setting, the femme fatale was portrayed as

You are crueller, you that we love,
Than hatred, hunger or death;
You have eyes and breasts like a dove,
And you kill men's hearts with a breath.

– Algernon Swinburne, "Satia Te Sanguine"

An illustration for the magazine *Ver Sacrum* by Ernst Stohr. (By permission of Victoria & Albert Museum, London/Art Resource, NY.)

malignant, threatening, and destructive, yet fascinating and alluring. The "agony of Romanticism" was what Percy Bysshe Shelley understood to be "the tempestuous loveliness of terror." Pleasure and pain, beauty and horror, life and death were combined to create not only an artistic sensibility but an artistic movement. The Romantics were not the first to express awe in the presence of the "beautifully horrid." What distinguishes the Romantics from earlier movements is the extent to which they translated this artistic sensibility into everyday life. Many of the poets, writers, and artists of this period lived sensational and flamboyant existences. Their poetry, as in the case of Algernon Swinburne, revealed their inner-most desires. Their emotional and sexual entanglements and often scandalous escapades—for example, Percy Bysshe Shelley leaving his wife for Mary Godwin Wollstonecraft, whose parents were both advocates of free love—were offered up for public consumption. The art and literature of the nineteenth century was the very definition of life imitating art and art imitating life.

The beautiful tragedy of the moth drawn to the flame *is* the Romantic ideal. In the earlier part of the nineteenth century, it was the fatal man who provided the flame. He was the sadist; his victim was a young, beautiful, and usually virginal woman. The fatal man was a romantic anti-hero, often dark, brooding and mysterious. His appearance and manners hinted at aristocracy, while his actions—especially toward women—wrought terror and destruction. In many ways, the fatal man was modeled after the poet Lord Byron. The scandalous events of his life, including affairs with married women, illegitimate pregnancies, and an incestuous affair with his half-sister Augusta, served to elevate Byron from the target of gossip, rumor, and disdain to a literary prototype. The Byronic hero—the fatal man whose latent vampiric qualities define his character—emerged as a literary convention that continues to be drawn upon today. By the end of the century, however, it was the male—by and large, the artist himself–who tended toward masochism. He was the moth about to be consumed by the fatal woman's flame. Two nineteenth century writers most influential in establishing the fatal woman as a literary type were the poets Charles Baudelaire and Algernon Charles Swinburne.

**In fact, to such an extent were Beauty and Death looked upon as sisters by the Romantics that they became fused into a sort of two-faced herm, filled with corruption and melancholy and fatal in its beauty—a beauty of which, the more bitter the taste, the more abundant the enjoyment.**

– Mario Praz, *The Romantic Agony*

*The Three Stages of Womanhood* by Edward Munch. Munch's sinister interpretation of the triple goddess of antiquity. Historical Museum, Bergen, Norway. (By permission of Scala/Art Resource, NY.)

Charles Baudelaire, a French poet who eventually died of syphilis, found great inspiration in images of love and death. An exceptional poet in his own right, Baudelaire also translated the works of Edgar Allan Poe into French. Like Poe, Baudelaire thought the death of a beautiful woman was one of the most poetic subjects in the world. The beauty of destruction and the pleasure of contamination are themes that run throughout Baudelaire's poetry. He sought his inspiration in affairs with women he perceived as cold and uncaring. Jeanne Duval, an actress, dancer and prostitute, was the subject of much of his poetry. Many of the poems in his most famous collection, *Les Fleurs du Mal*, were written with her in mind. Baudelaire's contemporaries remarked upon Duval's beauty but noted her generally pragmatic attitude toward her life and her livelihood. Yet in his poetry Baudelaire described her as a tigress, an implacable and cruel beast, a blood drinker, a demon without pity. Critic Mario Praz has described Baudelaire's "Metamorphosis of a Vampire"—a poem banned in France for its obscenity—as the crystallization of images of both the fatal man and the fatal woman. Regardless of Duval's true nature, she has come to be associated with the sadism that infuses Baudelaire's poetry. His celebration of cold and hard-hearted beauty, his fascination with the grim and the macabre, and his equation of lesbianism with the predatory female sowed the seeds for a literary fashion that would become a cliché by the end of the century.

Meanwhile, form her red mouth the woman, in husky tones,
Twisting her body like a serpent upon hot stones
And straining her white breasts from their imprisonment,
Let fall these words, as potent as a heavy scent:
"My lips are moist and yielding, and I know the way
To keep the antique demon of remorse at bay.
All sorrows die upon my bosom. I can make
Old men laugh happily as children for my sake.
For him who sees me naked in my tresses, I
Replace the sun, the moon, and all the stars of the sky!
Believe me, learned sir, I am so deeply skilled
That when I wind a lover in my soft arms, and yield
My breasts like two ripe fruits for his devouring–both
Shy and voluptuous, insatiable and loath–
Upon this bed that groans and sighs luxuriously
Even the impotent angels would be damned for me!"

When she had drained me of my very marrow, and cold
And weak, I turned to give her one more kiss–behold,
There at my side was nothing but a hideous
Putrescent thing, all faceless and exuding pus.
I closed my eyes and mercifully swooned till day:
And when I looked at morning for the beast of prey
Who seemed to have replenished her arteries from my own
The wan, disjointed fragments of a skeleton
Wagged up and down in a new posture where she had lain
Rattling with each convulsion like a weathervane
Or an old sign that creaks upon its bracket, right
Mournfully in the wind upon a winter's night.

– Charles Baudelaire, "Metamorphosis of a Vampire"
(translated by George Dillon and reprinted in
*Vampires, Wine and Roses*, edited by John Richard Stephens)

As influential in the development of the femme fatale was the British poet, Algernon Swinburne. An admirer of Baudelaire, Swinburne shared many of the same sensibilities. His fascination with images of harsh and distant women was not simply a literary device, but a personal avocation. A practicing masochist, Swinburne celebrated his sexual preferences in his writing. With poem titles such as "The Flogging Block," Swinburne came to be known, at least in certain circles, as a sort of champion of personal liberty. His poetry revealed his sexual preferences. Swinburne's female characters are "beautiful always beyond desire and cruel beyond words." Men are passive, love is martyrdom, and pleasure, pain. His remark on "the charms of birching" applies just as well to the primary theme of much of his writing: man as "the powerless victim of the furious rage of a beautiful woman."

Edward Munch's *The Vampire.* (By permission of Scala/Art Resource, NY.)

...out of death she kindles life; she uses the dust of man to strike her light upon; she feeds with fresh blood the innumerable insatiable mouths suckled at her milkless breast; she takes the pain of the whole world to sharpen the sense of vital pleasure in her limitless veins: she stabs and poisons, crushes and corrodes, yet cannot live and sin fast enough for the cruelty of her great desire. Behold, the ages of men are dead at her feet; the blood of the world is on her hands; and her desire is continually toward evil, that she may see the end of things which she hath made.

– Algernon Swinburne, in *Essays and Studies,* quoted in Mario Praz *The Romantic Agony*

Man, what have I to do with shame or thee?
I am not of one counsel with the gods.
I am their kin, I have strange blood in me,
I am not of their likeness nor of thine:
My veins are mixed, and therefore am I mad,
Yea therefore chafe and turn on mine own flesh,
Half of a woman made with half a god.

– Algernon Swinburne, *Fedra*

Swinburne's image of the femme fatale was also influenced by the works of the Pre-Raphaelites and notably Dante Gabriel Rossetti. Swinburne perhaps influenced Rossetti as much as Rossetti influenced him. Soon after Rossetti met Swinburne, he painted Lucrezia Borgia, one of Swinburne's favorite historical personages. Rossetti in some respects is a transitional figure in the development of the femme fatale. Themes of love and death are closely intertwined in his work, although much of his early work is more closely associated with the image of the Romantic heroine. One of Rossetti's most lasting contributions to the image of the femme fatale is the visual depiction of her beauty. Other artists interpreted the femme fatale, altering certain features and further developing her appearance, yet the images themselves recognizably descended from Rossetti's prototype. He based the women of his paintings on two models who were also the great loves of his life—Lizzie Siddal and Jane Morris. Both shared a heavy-lidded languor and melancholy expression. Their lush hair, sensuous lips, and strong jawline came to define the femme fatale. The near androgynous portrayal of these women—the columnar neck, pronounced jaw, and wide shoulders, set against dimished breasts, waist, and hips—remains common even today.

*Salome: The Dancer's Reward* by Aubrey Beardsley. Illustration for *Salome* by Oscar Wilde. (By permission of Victoria & Albert Museum, London/Art Resource, NY.)

One of the most enduring of the femme fatale's characteristics is her hair. Rossetti's love of a beautiful head of hair is well-documented, and the morbid fascination of being entangled in the tresses of a dangerous and seductive woman was no doubt fueled by the story of Rossetti burying early drafts of his poetry entwined in Lizzie Siddal's hair. Ten years later, when he opened her coffin to recover the poetry, the manuscript was so entangled it could not be removed without cutting her hair.

John Singer Sargeant's *Portrait of Madame Gautreau.* A similar painting, *Portrait of Madame X,* would be the inspiration for Rita Hayworth's satin gown in *Gilda* (1945). (By permission of the Tate Gallery/Art Resource, NY.)

> **And for you too, silent one who does not speak except to offend or to rave, for you too I represent knowledge.... Nothing is certain except cruelty and the hunger of the heart, and blood and tears, and the end of all things; and yet one does not know when is the time of weeping.**
>
> – Gabriele D'Annunzio's Isabella Inghirami in *Forse che si forse che no,* quoted in Mario Praz *The Romantic Agony*

Even in his later years, when illness drastically affected the quality of Rossetti's work and his ability to exhibit, his influence continued to spread. Edward Burne-Jones, a friend and disciple of Rossetti's (and, incidentally, father of Philip Burne-Jones, who would become famous for his painting "The Vampire") furthered the artistic representation of the femme fatale. Burne-Jones was attracted to what he called "exceedingly mischievous women," and at one point made several sketches and portraits of Florence Stoker, wife of Bram Stoker. As his style developed, Burne-Jones' images of women became increasingly slender, ethereal and brooding, in contrast to Rossetti's full-figured, voluptuous, and sensuous women. The androgynous quality hinted at in Rossetti's painting became more pronounced in

Burne-Jones' work, his women often bearing a striking resemblance to the male youths he also painted. The suppression of female curves, the slender, muscle-toned bodies, and the emphasis on melancholy facial expressions blurred distinctions between genders, just as the aggressive qualities of the femme fatale blurred the distinctions between "appropriate" male and female social behavior.

The slender, androgynous women of Burne-Jones were further refined and developed by the artist and illustrator Aubrey Beardsley. The strong jawlines, prominent chins, voluminous hair and elongated bodies were both a tribute to and a caricature of the style of the Pre-Raphaelites. Beardsley's most famous commission was Oscar Wilde's *Salome*. Salome was also the subject of some of the best-known and most characteristic works of the French artist Gustave Moreau. The artist's commentary on his painting *Salome in the Garden* highlights Moreau's attitude:

*The Climax* by Aubrey Beardsley. Illustration for Oscar Wilde's *Salome*. (By permission of Victoria & Albert Museum, London/Art Resource, NY.)

> This bored and fantastic woman, with her animal nature,giving herself the pleasure of seeing her enemy struck down, not a particularly keen one for her because she is so weary of having all her desires satisfied. This woman, walking nonchalantly in a vegetal, bestial manner, through the gardens that have just been stained by a horrible murder, which has frightened the executioner himself and made him flee distracted...

Edward Munch, a Symbolist painter whose work derived from that of Rossetti and Burne-Jones, portrayed women as blood-thirsty and himself as their victim. In Munch's *Salome*, the artist's disembodied head is entangled in Salome's hair. In *Vampire*, Munch is at the mercy of a red-headed demon, her mouth firmly affixed to his neck. It has been said that this woman is not meant to be a literal vampire, but a commentary on the vampire-like qualities of all women. Gustav Klimt, too, often expressed hostility toward any open display of women's sexuality, which he felt was the very antithesis to the ideal of Victorian womanhood. Although he is noted for ushering the femme fatale into the twentieth century, she had by this time gained such popularity that she no longer existed solely in the realm of "high" art.

The femme fatale gained her popularity in a time of great social change. The women's movement, which dates back to publication of Mary Wollstonecraft's *A Vindication of the Rights of Women* in 1792, gained momentum throughout the nineteenth century. The Women's Suffrage Movement put women's rights on the front page, as suffragists came face to face with police in public demonstrations, often ending up in prison. The anxiety many men felt toward women in the face of such demands for social change was reflected in the art, music and literature of the age.

Sarah Bernhardt on stage. (Photo courtesy of Michael Waltz, Nepenthes Productions.)

The femme fatale found an eager and enthusiastic audience among women who embraced her strength, boldness and sexual assertiveness. Women commissioned portraits of themselves looking "fashionably evil," and styles for clothing and jewelry emphasized the qualities of the femme fatale. Abundant hair and elaborate headdresses, gowns that accentuated broad shoulders and slim bodies, feather and fur accessories, jewelry in the form of stinging insects and writhing snakes—all added to the effect. Courtesans, actresses, dancers and singers adopted the image, and some succeeded so well they could be termed professional femmes fatales.

Sarah Bernhardt, the most famous actress of the era, adopted the role of the femme fatale in her much-publicized private life. Her carefully cultivated image included scandalous affairs, a luxurious lifestyle, and a penchant for the exotic and macabre (including the satin-lined coffin in which she liked to sleep). The playwright Sardou once said of Bernhardt, "If there's anything more remarkable than watching Sarah act, it's watching her live." Ida Rubenstein, a Russian dancer whose slender build and androgynous appearance resembled later paintings by Edward Burne-Jones, played the femme fatale both on stage and in her private life. At the height of her career, Claude Debussy, Gabriele D'Annunzio, and Léon Bakst collaborated in the creation of *The Martyrdom of Saint Sebastian*, while Rubenstein's lover, Romaine Brooks, immortalized her in a dark and sinister painting entitled *The Passing* (1911). In opera, the femme fatale could be found in Georges Bizet's *Carmen*, Richard Wagner's *Parsifal*, and Jules Massenet's *Manon*. But even on stage, the femme fatale soon became overused and anachronistic. The femme fatale soon moved on to a new art form: the Hollywood film.

Theda Bara in *Cleopatra* (1917).

6

# Theda Bara: Face of a Vampire, Heart of a Feministe

Her enigmatic stare helped to make Theda Bara a star. From *Cleopatra* (1917). (Photo courtesy of Michael Waltz, Nepenthes Productions.)

**She told her man, "Kiss me, my fool"—and he did! Her silent command cut through the rubble of Victorian sentiment like a stiletto and an enthralled America parroted her.**

– Marjorie Rosen, *Popcorn Venus*

In 1915, Theda Bara appeared in *A Fool There Was*, and overnight a screen sensation was born. Edward José starred as John Schuyler, a diplomat assigned a post in England. Theda Bara played the Vampire, the woman who, with a wake of fallen and broken men behind her, has set her sights on Schuyler. Schuyler leaves his wife and child and embarks on his journey to England. Unbeknownst to him, the Vampire has booked passage on the same ship. Through a variety of "chance" meetings, the Vampire succeeds in luring Schuyler not only from his wife and child, but also from his government post. He descends further into debauchery while his wife, ever faithful, waits patiently for his return. When Schuyler comes face to face with his wife, he is tempted to return to the happiness he once knew but is overcome by the Vampire's allure. All is foreshadowed in the opening credits, where Schuyler is represented as a man forced to choose between two beautiful roses in full bloom. In contrast, the Vampire looks disdainfully at the two roses in a vase before her. She picks up one of the two roses and, with apparent glee, crushes it in her hand.

*The Vampire* by Philip Burne-Jones.

**"In her dark eyes lurks the lure of the Vamp; in her every sinuous movement there is a pantherish suggestion that is wonderfully evil...."**

– Charles Dana Gibson, creator of the "Gibson Girl," on Theda Bara

In 1897, the same year as the publication of Bram Stoker's *Dracula*, Philip Burne-Jones exhibited his painting *The Vampire*. The painting was an expression of Burne-Jones' spurned love for the actress Mrs. Patrick Campbell. In the painting, a pale, black-haired woman, easily recognized as the well-known Mrs. Campbell, is shown with wild eyes and bared teeth, leaning over the collapsed and possibly dying body of the artist himself. In lieu of a description of the painting in the exhibit catalogue was a poem written by the artist's cousin, Rudyard Kipling, entitled "A Fool There Was."

The painting caused an immediate scandal, prompting Porter Emerson Browne to write a play about an all-consuming vampire woman. Browne turned the Fool of the poem into a Wall Street banker-turned-diplomat. The basic melodramatic ingredients were familiar to the audiences of the time: drinking, debt, and marital infidelity. A morality tale, the characters are listed in the credits as representatives of their societal roles: "The Husband," "The Wife," "The Little Girl." Infidelity appears as "The Vampire," the wanton woman who takes her pleasure in seducing and then destroying the man she has seduced.

Theda Bara do not pause,
For Vampires we adore;
And may the New Year
give you cause
To Vampire more and more!

– *Motion Picture,* 1917, quoted in Eve Golden's *Vamp*

This vampire, a classic femme fatale, destroyed her prey not through supernatural means but by luring him into cooperating with his own destruction. Although the other characters eventually are identified by name, the Vampire has no name. Her role as seductress overshadows her personality, history, and motivations. She is simply credited as "The Vampire." No questions are asked, and no explanations are necessary.

The play was first staged in the 1909–1910 season of the New York Liberty Theatre. It was an immediate hit. The popularity of the play and the obvious draw of the vampire character suggested to William Fox, founder of Fox Studios, that he had the makings of a monumental film. Fox consulted with the play's Broadway producer and leading man, Robert Hilliard, who told him that the actresses who played the vampire let success go to their heads and became impossible to work with. Hilliard advised Fox to find a relative unknown to play the part and to put her under contract. "The part will make her," he said.

Theda Bara, possibly as Juliet in *Romeo and Juliet* (1916). (Photo courtesy of Michael Waltz, Nepenthes Productions.)

Indeed the name Theda Bara was to become synonymous with the word "vampire."

Most girls are good, but good girls do not want to see other good girls on the screen. There's no interest, no fascination, in that for them. This is another reason for Miss Bara's success; she shows them something vastly different from the life they know. Few are either daring enough or desirous enough of leading a vampire existence, but through the medium of Theda Bara they can do her deed and live her life. Their emotions are enriched by just that much.

– Victor Freeburg, *Motion Picture,* April 1917, quoted in Eve Golden's *Vamp*

When Theodosia deCoppet (one of Theda's many stage names) was brought to Fox's attention, she was virtually unknown, despite many years of working on the New York stage. The facts of Theda Bara's life are so tied up with her rising stardom and the active imaginations of the movie studio publicity machine that it is still difficult to unravel the true story of Theodosia Goodman from the exotic tales of the dangerous and seductive Theda Bara. Among the discernible truths of Theodosia Goodman are that she was born in Cincinnati, Ohio in the 1880s (either 1880 or 1885), the child of Bernard Goodman, a Polish immigrant, and Pauline Louise Françoise deCoppet, a French wigmaker.

As a child, Bara showed an intense interest in acting. Her first performance was in a barn during her grade school years with her brother acting as bouncer (not, mind you, to keep people out, but to make sure the audience didn't dare leave—it helped that the two offered a bribe of free lemonade and cookies for everyone). In high school she was a member of the Dramatic Club and later continued her theater studies at the University of Cincinnati. In 1905, after two years at the university, Bara left Cincinnati for New York City to pursue an acting career. By 1910, she was playing second parts in the Yiddish theater on the Lower East Side. The following year, she landed a part in the touring company of a play called *The Quaker Girl*. By then, she was somewhat known as an ambitious actress with a talent for femme fatale roles. Still, her stage career had little momentum so, in 1914 she began her movie career.

A Fool there was and he made his prayer–
(Even as you and I.)
To a rag and a bone and a hank of hair–
(We called her the woman who did not care)
But the fool he called her his lady fair–
(Even as you and I.)

Oh, the years we waste and the tears we waste–
And the work of our head and hand
Belong to the woman who did not know–
(And now we know that she never could know)
And did not understand.

A Fool there was and his goods he spent–
(Even as you and I.)
Valor and faith and sure intent–
(And it wasn't the least what the lady meant)
But a fool must follow his natural bent
(Even as you and I.)

Oh, the toil we lost and the spoil we lost–
And the excellent things we planned
Belong to the woman who didn't know why–
(And now we know she never knew why)
And did not understand.

The Fool was stripped to his foolish hide–
(Even as you and I.)
Which she might have seen when she threw
him aside–
(But it isn't on record the lady tried)
So some of him lived but the most of him died–
(Even as you and I.)

But it isn't the shame, and it isn't the blame
That sting like a white hot brand–
It's coming to know that she never knew why–
(Seeing at last that she never knew why)
And could never understand.

– Rudyard Kipling, "A Fool There Was"

## [The vampire's desire] is a craving to love and be loved without counting the cost...a desire to be beautifully wicked.

– Theda Bara, *American Magazine*, 1920, quoted in Eve Golden's *Vamp*

Although it is said that she had many bit parts, her first recorded role was as a nameless face in the crowd in the film *The Stain*. It was in this film that Bara came to the attention of director Frank Powell who found in her a natural talent and a strong ability to take direction. Impressed by her skills and unable to afford a "real" star for his upcoming film *A Fool There Was*, he suggested to Fox that Bara be considered for the role of the vampire. Fox offered Bara the role.

The publicity department at Fox worked overtime in creating the public image of the woman who would become Bara. She was asked to review her childhood nicknames (Teddy, Theo, Theda) and the surnames of her parents and grandparents (Goodman, DeCoppet, Baranger). From this brainstorming session came Theda and Bara, short for Baranger. Years later, someone would hit on the fact that Theda Bara was also an anagram for Arab Death, a coincidence that gave both the publicity department at Fox and the movie industry media plenty of mileage.

Not wasting any opportunity to promote their new production and their new star, Fox Studios introduced Theda Bara to the press during a trip to Chicago. In a hotel room draped in "Egyptian" finery, copiously decorated with lilies and tuberoses and heavily scented with incense, the new screen sensation was introduced

Theda Bara in one of the costumes that would outrage the Women's Club of Omaha. The Club declared *Cleopatra* unfit for family viewing. (Photo courtesy of Michael Waltz, Nepenthes Productions.)

to the world. As the reporters awaited the appearance of this Arabian actress, the press agents told of her exotic origins. She was born in the sands of the Sahara, the only child of the French actress Theda de Lyse and Italian sculptor Giuseppe Bara. Or so they said. Bara had yet to appear. Then-aspiring journalist Louella Parsons noted that "the day was hotter than the proverbial hinges of the proverbial hot spot," yet Bara's press agent commented, "Miss Bara was born in the shadow of the sphinx, you know. It is very, very hot there and she is very cold." Bara appeared, draped in velvets and tiger-striped furs, pretending to speak little or no English. Bara took no questions but did deliver a prepared statement with a thick foreign accent. She described the character she plays in *A Fool There Was* as "a charnel house of men's dead hopes and withered ambitions...this vampire of mine possesses only one good or decent quality—her courage."

After the press conference the journalists were ushered out of the room. All except one. The young Louella Parsons was allowed to remain just long enough to see the "Arabian" star throw off her furs, throw open the window, and shout in a perfect Mid-western drawl, "Give me air!" And so, the mysterious Theda Bara, the creative collusion of an active and imaginative publicity department and a burgeoning media eager to give their readers something sensational, became the first studio star and one of the first silver screen legends.

"Theda played up her press conferences and interviews for all they were worth. At one point she declared herself the reborn spirit of a daughter of Seti, high priest of the Pharaohs, and was photographed at a museum gazing soulfully into the coffin of what she claimed was her own mummy." – Eve Golden, *Vamp*. (Photo courtesy Michael Waltz, Nepenthes Productions.)

**By 1918 Theda Bara was considered such an expert on vampires that she was subpoenaed to give "expert testimony on vampires and the psychology of vampiring" in a Los Angeles murder trial.**

– *Theda Bara: A Biography of the Silent Screen Vamp* by Ronald Genini

Until 1915, a "vamp" was either a piece of stage music performed between acts or the upper part of a shoe. After *A Fool There Was*, a vamp was a vampire, a wanton woman who seduces and destroys men. And vamp she did. Bara made movie after movie, forty-two movies in all, with forty of them between 1914–1919. Although she asked continually for other types of roles and did occasionally get them, audiences were less interested in the sympathetic roles she played in *Camille, Romeo and Juliet*, and *Kathleen Mavourneen*. Fans wanted to see her in the vamping roles celebrated in movie magazines and popular songs ("since Sarah saw Theda Bara, she's a wera, wera dangerous girl," was the refrain of one song).

Bara in a headdress reminiscent of Swinburne's description of a drawing by Michelangelo: "a head-dress of eastern fashion rather than western, but in effect made out of the artist's mind only; plaited in the likeness of closely-welded scales as of a chrysalid serpent, raised and waved and rounded in the likeness of a seashell." – Mario Praz, *The Romantic Agony*.

**"She's as bold as Theda Bara; Theda's bare but Becky's barer."**

– "Rebecca's Back from Mecca," a popular song from 1919 quoted in Eve Golden's *Vamp*

Bara's image owed a great deal to the turn of the century femme fatale. Her darkly-kohled and heavy-lidded eyes, her smoldering expression and abundance of hair, all classic attributes of the femme fatale, were accentuated and exaggerated. The names of her films read like a who's who of dangerous women: *Cleopatra*, Esmeralda in *The Hunchback, The Devil's Daughter, Sin, The Serpent, The Tiger Woman, Salome*, and *The Vixen*. Like Swinburne's description of Cleopatra, she was the woman with "electric hair, which looks as though it would hiss and glitter with sparks if once touched...wound up to a tuft with serpentine plaits."

The movies were entertainment for the masses, and the growth of the movie industry coincided with many social and political changes that defined the "modern" woman. Women could now vote. Victorianism was drawing its last breath. Expectations and mores were changing. So, too, were fashions—clothing allowed more mobility and more freedom. World War I, which brought women into the paid work force like never before, coincided with the height of Bara's popularity. She was one of the country's most successful spokespersons for Liberty Bonds, on one occasion selling more than three hundred thousand dollars worth in one afternoon. She set fashion trends—not, of course, in the gilded and veiled costumes she wore on-screen, but in the fashions she wore off-screen. One story relates how fans started a near riot in a department store trying to get their hands on a certain dress they had seen "The Vampire" admire. Store managers asked her not to shop at their stores for fear of the disruption she might cause. She also popularized the use of cosmetics, making the daily use of makeup by millions of women fashionable. "The Vampire" had influenced an entire generation.

There was a time when every studio had a vamp on its roster, sometimes two or three. Many have been forgotten over time, women such as Betty Blythe, Louise Glaum, Lya De Putti whose films featured garish costumes, melodramatic plots, and sensationalized characters. There were others who became Hollywood legends: Nita Naldi, the self-titled "Queen of the Vampires"; Pola Negri, the "Tempestuous Slav" and Rudolph Valentino's last love; and "Glorious" Gloria Swanson. But the mother of them all was the Vampire herself, Theda Bara.

Bara had so many imitators, she became a cliché. In the end, that cliché determined her fate. When Bara's contract expired in 1919, her box office appeal had already begun to decline. Her popularity outside of the studio was still high, but it relied more on the caricature of the vamp which had now become passé. The man-eating woman stereotype that defined her movies roles, was no longer a threat. At the same time, more modern acting styles (Bara was trained in the Delsarte method) and more sophisticated movie-making methods made Bara's staged performances seem arcane.

The traditional femme fatale had become outdated. On the eve of the jazz age, Bara's subversion of Victorian morality—she mocked all things considered decent in a very rigid and conservative era—was passé. Jazz babies—also called flappers and baby vamps—wore makeup and short-short skirts. They danced, they smoked, they drank. Hollywood had spawned a new generation of dangerous women.

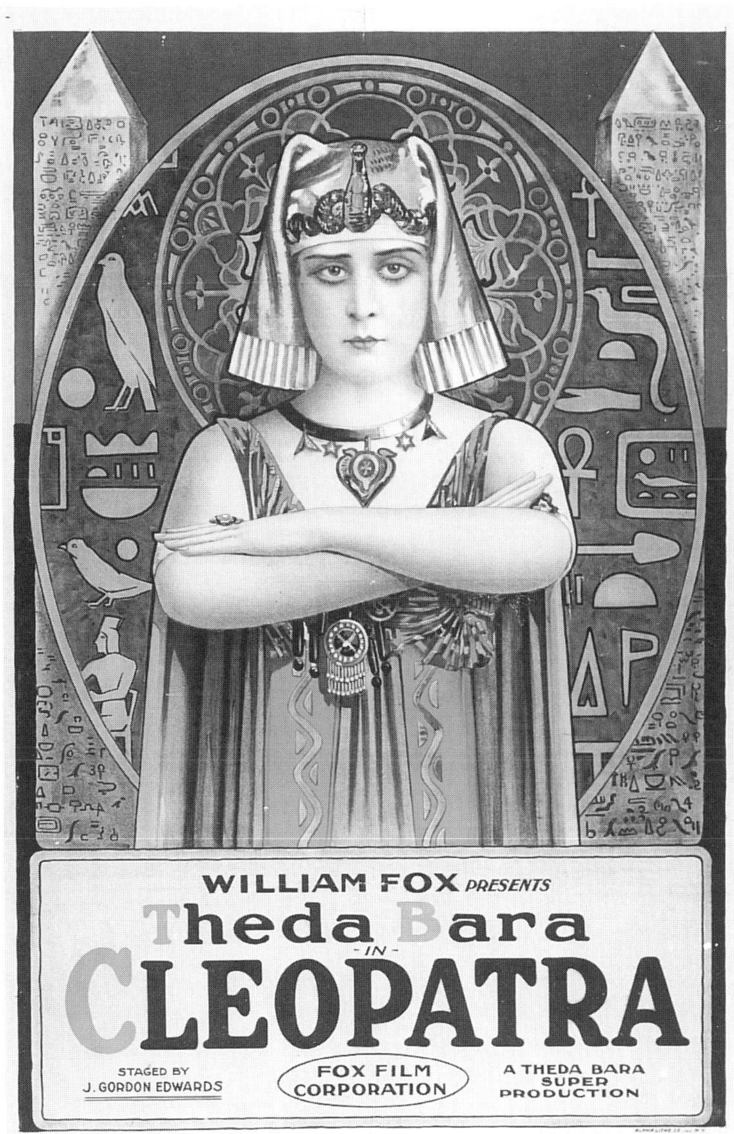


A poster for *Cleopatra*. The National Board of Review and the Ohio Board of Censors passed the film with no cuts. "The producers have followed history in a remarkable way, and Miss Bara's interpretation of the character is so skillfully and convincingly done that I feel justified in passing the picture as it was brought to the censor offices." – Mrs. Miller, Ohio's head Censor, in Eve Golden's *Vamp*. (Photo courtesy of Michael Waltz, Nepenthes Productions.)

**V stands for Vampire, and it stands for Vengeance. The vampire I play is the vengeance of my sex upon its exploiters. You see, I have the face of a vampire, perhaps, but the heart of a *feministe*.**

– Theda Bara quoted in *Virgins, Vamps, and Flappers* by Sumiko Higashi

Theda Bara as Cleopatra contemplating a lotus blossom.

Theda Bara's career as a film star was essentially finished by 1920, despite her fans' continued interest in her whereabouts, frequent articles in the press, and occasional rumors of a comeback. The effect of her style on the movie industry and her influence on the development of the femme fatale on the silver screen cannot be ignored, even by her detractors. Marjorie Rosen, author of *Popcorn Venus*, describes Bara's character as "an absurd sexual distortion" and "a permanent disservice to women." Even so, Rosen concedes that the "Bara school of exotics" transformed "motion picture sex into potent drawing power...reflecting a changing moral climate out of which postwar directors could make their statement freely, less hampered by social or sexual restrictions than ever before."

Theda Bara went on to live happily as a reigning member of the Beverly Hills social scene. She never forgot the essential elements that create a star. "People have always been hungry for glamour—they still are. But it takes showmanship and a constant sense of responsibility to hold their interest....[A star] should dress beautifully at all times....She must live their dreams for them and remain a figure of mystery. Glamour is the most essential part of Hollywood."

**As this man has done to me, so I will henceforth to all men. My heart is ice, my passion consuming fire. Let men beware.**

– *The Devil's Daughter*, quoted in *Theda Bara: A Biography of the Silent Screen Vamp* by Ronald Genini

Greta Garbo publicity shot.

# 7

# Sirens of the Silver Screen

## "I invented red toenails, I invented turbans, I invented boots. I wore boots in Poland, it was so cold. So I wore them in Hollywood."

– Pola Negri, *The New York Times,* 1970

By 1920, the Hollywood vamp had become a stock character, a cliché found not in the heavily-scented, tapestry-draped rooms of exotic locales, but in music halls, comedy revues, and Vaudeville routines. In fact, Theda Bara's last film, made in 1925, was not an ominous tale of insatiable hunger or a heart-wrenching drama of romantic entanglement, but a short film called *Madame Mystery,* directed by Stan Laurel and co-starring Oliver Hardy.

The true vampire, of course, is a survivor. She adapts to her surroundings, adjusting her needs and modifying her tactics as she goes. The 1920s brought a new femme fatale—younger, more vivacious, and more sexual.

The new Hollywood siren was bold and assertive, "masculine" in her desires and demands, yet "feminine" in her means of fulfilling them. Like her predecessors, she spelled danger and even death for the men who crossed her path. But unlike earlier vamps, her danger was well-camouflaged. The new femme fatale was just a bit softer, more tragic, and therefore more

Pola Negri in *The Cheat* (1923). The story concerns a society wife who gambles and loses ten thousand dollars. She then borrows money from a playboy, and when she tries to pay him back, he claims her by branding her. Two other versions were made, one in 1915 with Fanny Ward, the other in 1931 with Tallulah Bankhead.

sympathetic than her predecessors. And though her evil was diminished, her power and her appeal continued to ensnare audiences and create screen legends.

Just as the femme fatale had evolved to suit the demands of the time, so did the Hollywood star system. The United States' victory in World War I opened new markets for films and other exports. A growing international movie market and an economic boom in the United States permitted studios to cater to their favorite performers. Movie stars demanded bigger and bigger salaries, and studios who sought to keep their stars at "home" obliged. While Theda Bara's extravagant lifestyle was a facade, as much a performance as the roles she portrayed on film, the stars of the 1920s actually enjoyed the lush and luxurious lives that fans read about in movie magazines. The new femme fatale was not just an on-screen image; the role was played out in the opulent lives and decadent off-screen exploits of the rich and famous actresses who portrayed her.

Pola Negri, the first star to be "imported" by Hollywood, came to the United States from Poland in 1922. She arrived wearing a turban, Cossack dress, and high boots. Negri's hair, cut in the classic style of the flapper, her dark eyes, "exotic" speech, and extravagant clothing were every inch the femme fatale. She was called "The Wildcat" due to her fiery temper and the off-stage antics which kept her on the front pages of the movie magazines. Her thick accent, romantic past, and a failed marriage that left her with the title of Countess added to the mystery and allure that fueled her vamp image. Dressed to the nines, often in silks and sables, and more often than not with a glass of champagne in hand (no small feat during Prohibition), Negri lived the sumptuous life that Theda Bara was only rumored to have enjoyed. Negri was romantically linked to some of the most famous men of Hollywood. She had been engaged to Charlie Chaplin and intimately involved with Rudolph Valentino at the time of his death. Like Bara, she portrayed proud and tragic women such as Madame du Barry and Carmen in the films *Passion* and *Gypsy Blood*. Her film career, like Bara's, was short-lived. Although she would continue her making movies throughout her life, her star era came to a close with the end of her contract in 1928.

**"When I die, my epitaph should read: She Paid the Bills. That's the story of my private life."**

– Gloria Swanson, in Marjorie Rosen's *Popcorn Venus*

Negri's most fierce competitor was "Glorious" Gloria Swanson, who was already a reigning star at Paramount Pictures when Pola Negri arrived. Having started her film career as an extra at the age of fifteen in 1913, Swanson established herself in the Max Sennett comedies. In the last of her Sennett films, she appeared in a bathing suit and would be forever remembered as a former Max Sennett Bathing Beauty. Comedy, however, was not her preference. "I want to wring people's hearts and cry and die all over the place," she reportedly told Sennett when ending their association. Her elegance, demeanor, and style caught the eye of Cecil B. DeMille, who cast her with all of the trappings of the vamp—exotic headdresses, elegant gowns, and glittering jewels. Unlike Bara's vamp, Swanson's characterizations were essentially sympathetic, a femme fatale by circumstance. By the time she switched to Paramount in 1922, the vamp characterization had stuck, even though she went on to play a variety of roles at her new studio.

Swanson's lifestyle, like Negri's, widely surpassed Theda Bara's. Gloria Swanson could be seen wheeling down Sunset Boulevard in her leopard-upholstered Lancia, and her gold bathtub set in black marble was the envy of Hollywood's jet set. Her third marriage—to a man the studio assigned to her as an interpreter while working on a film in France—further enhanced her status: the young man was a Marquis, no less, and Gloria Swanson returned to Hollywood a Marquise.

**"I still am big. It's the pictures that got small."** – Norma Desmond, *Sunset Boulevard*

Like many of the movie queens of the silent era, Swanson left Hollywood and the motion picture industry with the advent of talking pictures. She did, however, return to make one more film. In 1949, she was asked by director Billy Wilder to do a screen test for a new film whose script was not yet finished. *Sunset Boulevard* was a mixture of eerie gothic and nostalgia for old Hollywood. Years later, author Danny Peary described the film:

> A woman from a long-forgotten age resides in self-imposed exile in a gloomy mansion in the hills. She still moves about although those who know of her insist she is dead. She is strong-willed, intelligent, and artistically gifted. She is alternately vain and self-despising; proud of her strength and capabilities but ashamed that she can't control her weaknesses: her destructive tendencies, her refusal to accept anyone not doing her bidding, and her jealousy toward "normal" women. It is her touch of melancholy and her woeful loneliness—no one is as out of place in the world—that makes her sympathetic despite her selfish, often cruel attitude and conduct. The only person who understands her is her peculiar man-servant....She asks the help of a man whose singular professional skills, she hopes, will help her enter the modern world....She is much older than he, but she falls in love with him....He is intrigued... but loves a woman his own age. She becomes jealous and tries to bring about an end to the relationship between him and the younger woman....When she realizes she has been deluded, the older woman tries to kill him....

"The story I have just told," he writes, "is, of course, a skeletal outline for Billy Wilder's *Sunset Boulevard*....It is also a skeletal outline for *Dracula's Daughter*...." *Sunset Boulevard* has been described as "the definitive Hollywood horror movie," and Norma Desmond as portrayed by Gloria Swanson is, without question, the classic vampire. She is a relic of a bygone era, yet someone who still has a curious elegance, a certain style, and a high-voltage personality. She attracts her unsuspecting victims like a spider in a web. Once caught, they will never again be truly free. Desmond drains the life from those around her until there is nothing left. And those who try to leave her find their only escape in death.

**"...he was conducting an investigation into his relations with women, with the object of conquering any passion that interfered with his passion for his work. He was not aroused by sexual love, which he dismissed as an enervating myth. It was sexual hate that engrossed his whole being with its flaming reality."**

– Louise Brooks on G. W. Pabst, director of *Pandora's Box*

*Sunset Boulevard* was Gloria Swanson's great comeback. The film was nominated for eleven Oscars in 1951, including a nomination for Swanson as Best Actress. Relative newcomer Judy Holliday would go on to win the Oscar, but Gloria Swanson—who will be forever remembered as the eccentric and unstable Norma Desmond–brought about a renewed interest in old movies and in the early, silent cinema.

Gloria Swanson in her final descent down the staircase in *Sunset Boulevard.*

## "No doubt the soul of Louise Brooks is not unlike the soul of Lulu—the hedonist without a sense of sin who lives for the moment and destroys men as she goes."

– William Shawn, *Lulu in Hollywood*

Louise Brooks was another silent movie actress who would define an era. With her bobbed hair, black bangs, and dancer's grace, Brooks was the epitome of the flapper. Her popularity was fueled by an innocence, youth and beauty that defined many of the characters that she played. In reality, she was warm, intelligent and spontaneous, having little patience for Hollywood's political games. When she was informed that her contract with Paramount would not be renewed, she went to Berlin to play Lulu in *Pandora's Box*, a role for which a young Marlene Dietrich had been considered. *Pandora's Box* is considered to be a classic film.

Louise Brooks as the widow in mourning in *Pandora's Box*.

*Pandora's Box* (1928), like *A Fool There Was*, began as a play. Written by German playwright Frank Wedekind, *Pandora's Box* and its companion piece, *Earth Spirit*, trace the story of Lulu from her adolescence to her tragic death. Lulu is seduced by a doctor and becomes his paramour. Dr. Schön, however, refuses to marry her, choosing a more socially-appropriate woman to be his wife. When his fiancée discovers the two lovers, Schön agrees to marry Lulu. On the evening after their wedding, he discovers Lulu with two other men and, assuming the worst, tells her she must kill herself to save her reputation and to preserve his. A struggle ensues, and a gun accidentally goes off, killing Schön. Lulu is tried for murder and found guilty. Lulu escapes from prison, aided by the Countess Geschwitz, one of the first lesbian characters in film. Lulu clearly bewitches women as well as men. The Countess stands out the only character in the film to help Lulu without asking anything in return. A tailspin follows in which each character is brought to a tragic end, all for the love of Lulu. She is finally reduced to prostitution to support her two male companions. Desperate for money, Lulu picks up her first client on Christmas Eve. He has no money, but he is kind, and Lulu takes him back to the garret where she lives. There she meets her final fate at the hands of Jack the Ripper.

Playwright Frank Wedekind, director G.W. Pabst and Louise Brooks expanded on the traditional vamp/femme fatale by creating a happy, sensual, likable and warm-hearted Lulu. She is not driven by anger, revenge or cynicism, and unlike previous movie vamps, takes no pleasure in destroying others. Lulu is motivated by pleasure for its own sake and driven by her own sexual desires. The innocence and recklessness with which she pursues these desires makes her a tragic figure. She has no concept of sin nor does she wish to cause harm. Her very presence—her animal magnetism—brings those around her to their ultimate demise. Lulu suffers because Schön cannot control his jealousy, Alwa can't control his gambling, Schigolch cannot control his alcoholism, Rodrigo and Casti-Piani can't control their greed, and Jack the Ripper cannot control his psychosis. Each one of these men condemns Lulu, whose beauty and vivaciousness bring out the base and petty desires of men.

*Pandora's Box* was thoroughly panned by critics and heavily censored. *Diary of a Lost Girl*, also directed by Pabst and starring Louise Brooks, received the same poor reception a year later. The sexually-explicit themes, daring content (specifically a scene in which Lulu dances with the Countess Geschwitz), and the fact that Hollywood no longer imported subtitled films sealed the fate of films such as these. Despite the fact that they were buried and forgotten by the viewing public, *Pandora's Box* and *Diary of a Lost Girl* marked a significant shift in the portrayal of the femme fatale. The new femmes fatales, like Lulu, were victims of circumstance, not villains. And their fate, although not always as dramatic as Lulu's demise, would be tragic.

**"...if it were not for your big brown childlike eyes, I should be forced to regard you as the most designing bitch that ever brought a man to ruin."**

**"I only wish I were."**

– Alwa and Lulu, in the play *Pandora's Box*

Joan Crawford captured the tone and style of the Jazz Age. The jazz baby, also known as the baby vamp, had taken on the mantle of the femme fatale. Although largely remembered as a stern and imposing diva in both her public and private life, Crawford's first starring roles were as dynamic and impetuous dancing girls in the 1920s. Dancing girls were the epitome of the Jazz Age, and every well-known actress of the era had at least one chorine role. Joan Crawford's big dream was to be a dancer, and when first approached about being an actress she said she wasn't interested. But when offered work in Hollywood at a starting salary of seventy-five dollars per week, Crawford, who had been working since the age of eleven, and her mother, a laundress, couldn't refuse. Crawford's dancing talents and her vivacious screen presence landed her several chorine roles, but it was her role as Diana Medford in *Our Dancing Daughters* (1928) that made her a star.

Betty Boop is best remembered for her red-hot jazz baby persona. With a head like a giant peanut, vast mascara'd eyes, too-kissable lips, baby-doll voice (courtesy of Helen Kane), flattened marcelled hair, and mere threads of a dress exposing miles of hot flesh, she was the perfect celluloid sex toy.

– Gary Morris, *Bright Lights Film Journal*

The jazz baby, like the vamp before her, had lost her ability to shock audiences. By the 1930s, the flapper had become commonplace, and she, too, became little more than a cliché. Once a symbol of reckless youth running rampant, the jazz baby literally became a cartoon character. Betty Boop, with her "boop-boop-a-doop," offered more than a little sexual innuendo, yet she was sweet and endearing. No longer threatening to the image of the "good" girl, the jazz baby, like the vamp, evolved with the times.

And so did Joan Crawford. From her roles as an empty-headed-but-sincere hedonist, she went on to films which cast her as the working girl who—through hard work, dedication and a certain amount of sex appeal—makes good by marrying the hero. She was extremely popular with American audiences, young women who saw themselves in the characters she played and saw their hopes in her success as a "shopgirl" who had become a star. But her range as an actress was minimal, and the studio had little idea how to use her talents. Although she worked steadily throughout her years with MGM, she was given little choice of roles, and many of her scripts were fashioned out of unpublished plays, magazine short stories or novels the studio had bought years earlier and forgotten. The weak story lines and disappointing build-up gave critics the opportunity to dissect her talents, although her fans were as loyal as ever. In 1943, disappointed by MGM's disinterest in her career, she chose to leave the studio and to work independently. Her first project after leaving the studio was *Mildred Pierce*, a film adapted from the novel by James Cain. (1945).

She put on a show wherever she went. At a wedding, she was the bride. At a funeral, she was the corpse.

– Dorothy Manners, in *Joan Crawford: A Biography*

In *Mildred Pierce*, Crawford plays the hard-working divorced mother of a spoiled daughter who steals her mother's lover. Crawford gave her best performance to date and won her first Oscar for Best Actress. As much as she desired this recognition, *Mildred Pierce* also marked a definitive turn in her career. Approaching her fifties, Crawford would never again play the ingenue. From 1945 until her last film in 1967, she was typecast as the overbearing, castrating woman. This demonization would show itself in her real life, too, as she became increasingly eccentric and volatile and more and more dependent on alcohol. The Joan Crawford many fans remember is the cruel mother of *Mommy Dearest*, her daughter Christina's tell-all autobiography revealing the years of abuse she and her siblings endured living with the woman once named "Queen of the Movies."

Joan Crawford in an early publicity shot.

**There is one thing about Crawford you must admire: her ability to create a myth, a legend about herself.**

– Sterling Hayden, her co-star in *Johnny Guitar*, as quoted in *Joan Crawford: A Biography* by Bob Thomas

About the time that Crawford's star began to fall at MGM, Bette Davis' star began to rise. Davis had been groomed for the stage at a very early age by her mother, Ruth Favor Davis. Drama lessons, dance lessons, and roles in community theater and school plays helped to prepare Davis for Hollywood. She wasn't beautiful in the typical, starlet sense, and her performances on screen were atypical as well. When Davis began her screen career, most established actors had been influenced by the era of silent film. Without the tendency towards melodrama and overacting that characterized much of the silent era and the decade that followed, Davis paved the way for more realistic portrayals on film.

**I think that Bette Davis would probably be burned as a witch if she had lived two or three hundred years ago. She gives the curious feeling of being charged with power which can find no ordinary outlet.**

– English critic Arnot Robertson in Whitney Stine's *Mother Goddam: The Story of the Career of Bette Davis*

Bette Davis.

Davis played a variety of minor roles at Warner Brothers in the early years of her career. Often cast as the gangster's romantic interest, she made the most of any opportunity to put her talents to the test. When RKO offered her the chance to star as Mildred in the film adaptation of Somerset Maugham's *Of Human Bondage* (1934), Davis, under a strict contract for Warner Brothers, immediately requested that she be "loaned" to RKO to make the film. As the tough-talking, explosive and abusive Mildred, Davis gave her best performance to date. Following that performance, and her subsequent Academy Award for her role in *Dangerous* (1935), Davis challenged what she considered to be unfair restrictions placed on her as a contract player for Warner Brothers. Davis pursued legal action against the studio. Although her chal lenge was denied, her bold stance, her outspoken criticism of the Hollywood system, and the intransigence of her position bolstered the Davis legend.

Like Crawford, Davis continued working until the end of her life. Her staccato gestures, chain-smoking, and distinctive speaking style made her a favorite among impersonators. Best known for the role of the fragile yet outspoken Margo Channing in *All About Eve* (1950), she continued to play the diva until the end.

Equally important in the development of the screen diva are Greta Garbo and Marlene Dietrich. Both were groomed for stardom. Garbo and Dietrich shared an air of mystery, a passionate sensibility that suggested a private intensity and the possibility of possession. Unlike the vamp who voraciously pursued and consumed men, this femme fatale drew men to her like the mythical Circe. And like the sailors who followed Circe's song, men found themselves sacrificing everything for an unattainable love.

**We are taught that to be "shameless" is the worst thing, but it isn't until one loses one's shame that one is really free.**

– Bette Davis in *Bette Davis Speaks* by Boze Hadleigh

Garbo's screen presence, like Theda Bara's, was steeped in foreign mystique. But unlike Bara's, Garbo's foreign mystique was genuine. Born in Sweden, she had been brought to Hollywood in 1925 by her mentor, director Mauritz Stiller. Producer Irving Thalberg cast Garbo in her first Hollywood film opposite Ricardo Cortez, a Valentino-like studio star. Commenting on her role in *The Torrent*, Garbo said, "I do not want to be a silly temptress. I cannot see any sense in getting dressed up and doing nothing but tempting men in pictures." But audiences loved her and wanted more. Garbo brought a subtlety and sophistication to her roles that added an ambiguous quality to the femme fatale. She was passionate and forceful and as likely to reject a suitor as to submit to his advances. She was fatal but not evil. She knew that love ends in tragedy. It was this portrayal of the femme fatale whose love catches men in the web of her circumstances that ultimately came to define Garbo's screen persona.

Marlene Dietrich's portrayal of the woman of mystery was perhaps more familiar to American audiences. Her characters were more calculating and more assertive than Garbo's. Dietrich debuted her manipulative on-screen persona in her first starring role, as Lola Lola in *The Blue Angel*.

Early in her career, Dietrich had been passed over by G.W. Pabst for the role of Lulu in *Pandora's Box*. Pabst later said that Dietrich was "too old and too obvious [to play Lulu]–one sexy look and the picture would have become a burlesque." Not long afterward, Dietrich would meet her mentor, director Josef von Sternberg. She would be von Sternberg's Lola Lola, the femme fatale of *The Blue Angel*. But first, the director ordered her to lose weight, advised her on fashion and makeup, and rehearsed every glance and inflection that would make her the film's dark angel. In *The Blue Angel*, veteran actor Emil Jannings played an aging professor who becomes enchanted with Lola Lola, a cabaret singer. She taunts the professor, teasing him only to humiliate him again and again. Lola Lola enjoys her power and delights in his pathetic devotion to her. The success of *The Blue Angel* brought both von Sternberg and Dietrich to Hollywood, where he would direct her next six films, including *Morocco*, *Blonde Venus*, and *The Devil is a Woman*.

The sirens of the 1930s and 1940s, stripped of the unnatural power of Theda Bara's predatory style or the animal instinct of Louise Brooks' Lulu, soon lost their edge altogether. The whore with a heart of gold, the sinner who is really a saint, the nurturing mother inside Everywoman replaced the classic vamp, removing a

Greta Garbo as the double-crossing spy in *Mata Hari* (1932).

sinister quality from women's sexuality. Sex was no longer the domain of "bad" girls alone. "Pin-ups," cheesecake photos of actresses published in military magazines during World War II, helped publicize movies and were considered to be morale boosters. Hugh Hefner described them as "friendly reminders to the boys away from home of what—and whom—we were fighting for."

**...she could be anything, the Queen of Society or a tramp, or all the mysterious women in history. Whatever you like, it's all there.**

– Director Allan Dwan in John Kobal's *Rita Hayworth: The Time, the Place and the Woman*

Betty Grable, Veronica Lake, Lana Turner, and Rita Hayworth were popular pin-up girls during the war, and all had successful careers throughout the 1940s and into the 1950s, but it was Rita Hayworth who really embodied the qualities of the sex goddess of the time. As Rita Cansino, she began her career as a dancer with her father, Eduardo, as her partner. She enjoyed a successful film career throughout the 1930s, first as a starlet and later in more dynamic roles. In *Blood and Sand* (1942), Hayworth starred as Doña Sol, the fiery Latina temptress who destroys the bullfighter Juan Gallardo, played by Tyrone Power.

Marlene Dietrich in *The Blue Angel* (1930). (Photo courtesy Forrest J Ackerman.)

Rita Hayworth singing "Put the Blame on Mame" in *Gilda* (1945).

## "They married Gilda, but they woke up with me."

– Rita Hayworth in Marjorie Rosen's *Popcorn Venus*

Hayworth's star power was further enhanced by World War II. When the United States entered the war after the bombing of Pearl Harbor, so did Hollywood. Movies celebrated U.S. action in the war. At the Hollywood Canteen in Los Angeles and the Stage Door Canteen in New York, soldiers on leave could meet their favorite stars, and both locations were celebrated in popular Hollywood films (*Hollywood Canteen* in 1944 and *Stage Door Canteen* in 1943) that introduced the idea of an "all-star" cast. Both "pin-up" and "cheesecake" entered the nation's vocabulary, and popular stars did their part to "cheer" the boys on the front lines. A photo of Hayworth wearing a black lace negligee and kneeling on a bed became an instant favorite, surpassed only by the photo of Betty Grable in a white bathing suit. Hayworth became *Life* magazine's favorite cover girl—the magazine named her the Love Goddess. She made a number of films, including musicals such as *Tonight and Every Night* with Fred Astaire, but it was as the Love Goddess that Hayworth would truly make her mark. In 1945, working with her then-husband Orson Welles, Hayworth starred in *Gilda*. Hayworth melted the screen, forever emblazoning her image in movie history with an unforgettable song-and-dance number. In a strapless black satin evening gown and elbow length gloves, Gilda performs a striptease designed to both entice and humiliate her husband Johnny (played by Glenn Ford) while singing "Put the Blame on Mame." Every Hayworth role thereafter would be a variation on Gilda.

Hayworth left Hollywood at the height of her career in 1949 to marry Prince Aly Khan, spiritual leader of the Ismailis and reputedly the richest man in the world at the time. After her divorce in 1951, she returned to make many more films, but by that time there was a new sex goddess on the horizon. Her name was Marilyn Monroe.

## I can be smart when it's important, but most men don't like it.

– Marilyn Monroe as Lorelei in *Gentlemen Prefer Blondes* (1953)

Marilyn Monroe in a black negligee, emphasizing her sex appeal while downplaying the "girl next door" persona for which she became famous.

If the forties were the decade of the pin-up, the fifties were the decade of the playmate. Hugh Hefner, inspired by the "pin-ups" of his army days and the "good girl art" featured in most men's magazines, decided he wanted to be the purveyor of a magazine that celebrated "the wholesomeness of the girl next door, but acknowledged her sexuality as well." Hefner began work on *Stag Party*, a magazine dedicated to the sexual aspect of "the girl next door." It wasn't until the second issue that Hefner began using the title *Playboy*. Short on funds for photography, he bought reprint rights from a calendar company. Among the photos he purchased was the now-famous nude photo of Marilyn Monroe, "Golden Dreams." A Sweetheart of the Month, Monroe was renamed Miss December 1953.

Marilyn Monroe, born Norma Jean Baker in 1926, began her career as a model. She began her acting career at Twentieth Century-Fox, where she played sexy blondes who use their sexuality to get what they want. Monroe carefully cultivated the on-screen persona that culminated in the character of Lorelei Lee in *Gentlemen Prefer Blondes* (1953). Lorelei and her partner Dorothy (Jane Russell) are entertainers in pursuit of husbands. Lorelei's character is identified with the song "Diamonds Are a Girl's Best Friend," a song that made both the movie and

Monroe famous. The song is both a parody and a celebration of the child/woman who is both Lorelei and Monroe. The implicit message is that by behaving the way men want them to behave, women, like children, can get what they want. The success of *Gentlemen Prefer Blondes* established Monroe as a sex goddess, and the boundaries between the person and the symbol became harder and harder to draw.

"She felt, however, like two people; the neglected Norma Jean and some new being who belonged to the ocean and the sky and the whole world." - Carl E. Rollyson Jr. in *Marilyn Monroe, A Life of the Actress.*

**With a soft-spoken voice, helpless as a sharp knife, her eyes at half-mast like a cobra watching its prey, she was a cruel child tearing off butterfly wings—gay, mean, proud and inscrutable.**

– Jean Negulesco, director of *How To Marry a Millionaire,* in Carl Rollyson's *Marilyn Monroe: A Life of the Actress*

Marilyn Monroe exuded an overt sexuality and intense eroticism cushioned by a girlish naïveté, the vamp who lived next door. This pairing of opposites—carnal knowledge and innocence—redefined the femme fatale for a new generation of moviegoers. She was an amalgam of archetypes. Like Theda Bara, she maintained a heady sexuality that brought men to their knees. Like Louise Brooks, she projected a naïveté about her sexual persona. Like Greta Garbo and Marlene Dietrich, she had a mysterious, unknowable quality that allowed others to project their own desires onto her. This amalgam of popular feminine archetypes—and her untimely death—catapulted Marilyn Monroe from popular icon to American legend.

By the late 1950s, the vamp as cruel and heartless man-eater was largely forgotten, a relic of some ancient past. Men's magazines like *Playboy* popularized the notion that even good girls enjoy sex. The vamp in the form of the sex kitten was no longer threatening because she had, in fact, been tamed. In 1958, screenwriter Anita Loos described the vamp as "a girl who is intrigued by a member of the opposite sex, to a point where she will make an effort to please him." On the eve of the sexual revolution, overtly sexual women were not so shocking. To portray her as such was as anachronistic as Theda Bara's vamp in the jazz age. To be truly shocking, her sexuality had to have an edge. The femme fatale evolved once again. As always, her power was in her sexuality, an evil, deadly sexuality beyond all constraint. This time, she arose in the form of the vampire.

Angelica Huston as Morticia in *The Addam's Family* (1991).

# 8

# "Cinderella in a Nightmare.": The Allure of the Female Vampire

Actresses who played vamps—Swanson, Crawford, and Garbo—are remembered for their extravagant personalities, passion, and style, and of course, for the remarkable characters they brought to life. But women who appeared on-screen as vampires are often remembered only as the characters they played. We remember Carmilla, Countess Zaleska and the Brides of Dracula long after we have forgotten the names of the actresses who played them.

Carl Dreyer's 1932 *Vampyr* was the first attempt to translate Sheridan LeFanu's "Carmilla" to the screen. *Vampyr* tells the story of a young man who witnesses an old woman's attack on two young sisters. In the film, which has a dream-like quality, the old woman, Carmilla, more closely resembles the witches of classic fairy

The vampire hag of Carl Dreyer's *Vampyr* (1932). (Photo courtesy of Forrest J Ackerman.)

tales than the slender, languorous young woman of LeFanu's tale or the serpentine Geraldine of Coleridge's "Christabel." Rather, the haggard, blood-sucking witch is reminiscent of the warnings against wicked women contained in the *Malleus Maleficarum*.

Lon Chaney and Edna Tichenor in *London After Midnight* (1922). (Photo courtesy of Forrest J Ackerman.)

Although vampire films date as far back as the 1890s, few of the early films have survived. Tod Browning's *London After Midnight* (1922), starring Lon Chaney, is one of the most famous "lost" vampire films. Browning directed three of the most famous of the classic vampire movies, and his image of the vampiric woman would influence the representation of women vampires for decades. In *London After Midnight*, Edna Tichenor's vampire wears a negligee-like shroud. Her thick, dark hair is pulled back from her face to reveal dark, kohled eyes. This coldly impassive portrayal of the vampire in *London After Midnight* would be seen again in the images of the brides in *Dracula* (1931) and in *Mark of the Vampire* (1935).

The three women who inhabit the bowels of Castle Dracula in Stoker's novel appeared only briefly in Browning's film version of *Dracula*. Their eerie presence, slow-moving pace and stalking motions emphasized the animal-like qualities attributed to vampires and predatory women alike. It was Carroll Borland, however, in her role as Luna in *Mark of the Vampire*, who would define the look, style, and qualities of female vampires in film for generations.

**It is not only the male you must fear. There is, it is said, at the castle, that which is worse: a woman—for a woman should give life, not take it—and when a woman is of the Devil, that is worse than the Devil himself.**

– Carroll Borland, *Countess Dracula*

Carroll Borland in *Mark of the Vampire* (1935). "In the book," Borland explained, "it says that Lucy turned around and her face looked like a Japanese mask...and she hissed like an angry cat...." Quoted in *Countess Dracula*. (Photo courtesy of Forrest J Ackerman).

Carroll Borland first saw Bela Lugosi in a 1928 stage production of *Dracula*. She was so enthralled with the actor and his Count Dracula that she began writing a novel, one in which a contemporary woman meets the Count fifty years after his alleged demise in the novel. The young Carroll Borland wrote Lugosi about her sequel. He invited her to his hotel, and the two began a life-long friendship which would launch Borland's career in the theater. In 1934, Carroll Borland asked Lugosi for the chance to play the role of Dracula's daughter in the remake of *London After Midnight*, tentatively titled *Vampires of Prague*. Once cast, the studio publicized Borland's role as "Cinderella in a nightmare."

Borland worked with Bill Tuttle, then a makeup apprentice, to develop Luna's appearance. Adapting Lugosi's face with her long, dark lashes, luminescent eyes, and straight hair, Borland established a classic vampire look. Her contribution went beyond hair and makeup. In a crucial scene, where Luna is captured and is about to bite Irena in the neck, Browning directed Borland to "turn around, snarl like a wolf and growl." Borland, a fan of the novel *Dracula*, disagreed. "In the book," she explained, "it says that Lucy turned around, and her face looked like a Japanese mask… and she hissed like an angry cat…." With this single gesture, the passive vampire woman acquired a depth and ferocity never before seen on film. The vampire women of *London After Midnight* and *Dracula*, though ominous, were nevertheless quiet, impervious, and generally relegated to the sidelines. With a single cat-like noise and a threatening gesture, Carroll Borland established Luna as a force to be reckoned with, equal in malice to Count Mora, and created a look as recognizable and long-lived as Lugosi's.

*Dracula's Daughter*, the 1936 sequel to Bela Lugosi's *Dracula*, was the first vampire film to present a central woman character, the Countess Zaleska. *Dracula's Daughter* also featured a lesbian attraction so prominent that the studio feared censorship unless the lesbian overtones were diminished. The sexual desire expressed by the Countess as the young model, Maria, portrayed by Nan Grey, pulls the clothing from her own shoulders is unmistakable. This is, without question, the most erotically charged sequence in the entire film.

Gloria Holden as the Countess Zaleska mourning her father's death and her vampiric condition in *Dracula's Daughter* (1936). (Photo courtesy of Forrest J Ackerman.)

## "Save the women of London from *Dracula's Daughter*."

– Movie poster

*Dracula's Daughter* was rather freely adapted from an excised chapter of Bram Stoker's novel. Gloria Holden's Countess Zaleska is a daughter mourning her father's death. She is tall, refined and elegant, very much in the aristocratic tradition of Bela Lugosi's Count Dracula. What is particularly striking is the remarkable resemblance which the mourning Countess shares with religious iconography of the Virgin Mary. Countess Zaleska, unlike most film vampires who precede and follow her, is deeply aware of her curse and desperately wishes to escape her fate. She is a woman suffering, much like the traditional images of the Virgin Mary. The Countess' knowledge and compulsions, however, relegate her to be eternally damned. Despite her efforts to be cured, she ends, as many vampires do, with a stake through her heart.

Louise Allbritton and Lon Chaney Jr. in *Son of Dracula*. (Photo courtesy of Forrest J Ackerman.)

In *Son of Dracula* (1942) Louise Allbritton plays a pivotal role as Katherine Caldwell, the first movie vampire victim who is happy to be bitten. Count Alucard (Lon Chaney, Jr.) follows Caldwell to her home in the Louisiana bayou to make her his vampire bride. She has no qualms about becoming a vampire and, in fact, looks forward to the transformation with gusto. Unfortunately, she dies before her final transformation. Alucard is shot with an ordinary bullet that passes through him, killing her instead.

## In her eyes desire! In her veins the blood of—a monster!

– Movie Poster, *Blood of Dracula*

In the 1950s, vampires were embraced by a new generation of viewers. Teenagers were enjoying a revival of old horror films, and new vampire films were being made with a teenage audience in mind. In *Blood of Dracula* (1957), Sandra Harrison plays a depressed and neglected teenager sent to boarding school by her father and his new wife. The teen's outsider status and lack of friends make her a perfect guinea pig for her female biology teacher whose research has been ignored by the male academic establishment. The teacher administers a serum that turns the student into a bloodthirsty beast, complete with fangs, pronounced body hair, and a Neanderthal-like brow. Harrison's victims are teenagers from the neighboring all-boys school. Although this destructive power aligns the character with the classic femme fatale, the story relates more to the werewolf than the vampire.

Nevertheless, the film's subtext belies all of the conventional B-movie trappings. Not only does *Blood of Dracula* include a critique of sexism in the academic establishment (particularly the glass ceiling for women in the sciences) and the dysfunction of the American family, the movie also highlights a nascent lesbianism, a schoolgirl's crush on an attentive teacher. *Blood of Dracula* has more than a little in common with the lesbian film classic, *Mädchen en Uniform* (1931).

The sexual themes of *Blood of Dracula* foreshadowed an increasing interest in lesbian vampires and women as central characters in vampire films. Of course, many lesbian roles were secondary characters, often passive victims recruited through the force of seduction into the legions of the night. But a more tolerant attitude toward sexuality and "swinging" allowed directors to challenge studio censorship. Horror, science fiction, and fantasy films—already marginalized as genre pictures—pushed the limits of acceptable behavior in ways mainstream movies could not and would not. These films paved the way for more explicit representation of both sexuality and violence in mainstream culture, thereby diminishing the role of censors. It was in this atmosphere of burgeoning sex and violence that vampire movies flourished.

Hammer Studios stepped into the limelight, setting the tone for the elegant, sexy horror film. The British production company had been making films since the 1930s, including *The Mystery of the Marie Celeste* (1936), released in the United States as *The Phantom Ship*, starring Bela Lugosi. In the late 1950s, Hammer became known primarily for its horror films, which owed their popularity to the studio's overt portrayal of the sexual underpinnings of the vampire myth.

Sandra Harrison and Louise Lewis in the teacher's office in *Blood of Dracula*. (Photo courtesy of Forrest J Ackerman.)

Andree Melly looking particularly enthusiastic in *Brides of Dracula* (1960). (Photo courtesy of Forrest J Ackerman.)

Following the success of the studios' first horror production, *The Curse of Frankenstein*, Hammer quickly moved on to Bram Stoker's *Dracula* (1958), released in the United States as *Horror of Dracula*. Christopher Lee, donning Dracula's cape and eschewing the Frankenstein makeup he wore for *The Curse of Frankenstein*, emerged as the definitive sexually-charged, virile vampire. Bright colors and lush, opulent sets lent an air of decadence to the film. *Horror of Dracula* was much more explicit than any other vampire film to date, both in terms of sex and bloodshed. Dracula's victims clearly enjoyed being bitten—the sharp intake of breath and the ethereal stare in their eyes highlighted the sensual nature of the vampire's kiss.

The women of Hammer horror films were portrayed just as erotically as Christopher Lee's Count Dracula. *Brides of Dracula* (1960) features a naïve French governess who falls for a vampire. David Peel plays Baron Meinster, whose mother, aware of her son's condition but unable to have him killed, keeps him chained up in a locked room. She brings him the victims he needs to survive. When a naïve French governess is stranded in the mansion, he begs her to unlock the chains. Touched by his appeal, she releases him, setting him free to prey on the girls' school where she is to teach. Although it was ten years before women would take center stage in Hammer's vampire movies, the overt sexuality of the vampire women in both *Dracula* and *Brides of Dracula* became part and parcel of the Hammer "formula." Sexy vampire women featured prominently in *Kiss of the Vampire* (1964), *Dracula: Prince of Darkness* (1966), *Dracula has Risen from the Grave*,(1968) and *The Satanic Rites of Dracula* (1973).

The seventies saw a number of films based on classic female vampires, particularly Carmilla and the Countess Bathory. Combining the eroticism of the original stories, the lavishness of Hammer, and overt lesbian plots, these films became cult classics among women and men alike. European actresses like Ingrid Pitt, Yutte Stensgaard, and Delphine Seyrig ushered in the "Golden Age of Lesbian Vampires"—ensuring its own chapter in this book and in vampire movie history.

Meanwhile, in the United States, the films *Count Yorga, Vampire* (1970) and *Return of Count Yorga* (1971) boasted a bevy of beautiful ladies initiated into the world of the undead by the sophisticated and aloof Count Yorga—who has left his Transylvanian castle for the urban wilderness of Los Angeles. One by one, the women of both *Count Yorga, Vampire* and *Return of Count Yorga* are bitten, and in time, turn on the men who had been their husbands, boyfriends, or lovers in life.

Barbara Steele as Princess Katia from *Black Sunday* (1960). She could just as easily be the Goddess Hel who, with her dogs, guards the gates to the Underworld. (Photo courtesy Forrest J Ackerman.)

Not all the women vampires of this period appeared as members of the male vampire's harem. The vampiric witch Princess Ada is the protagonist of *Black Sunday* (1960), directed by Mario Bava and starring Barbara Steele. The film begins in the seventeenth century with Princess Ada and her consort being whipped by a frenzied mob determined to rid their village of the source of witchcraft that has plagued the town. An indignant Ada curses them all and swears her revenge. The villagers, convinced of their victory over the witch, secure the mask of the demon, lined with spikes, by driving it into her face. The film then cuts to the nineteenth century where two physicians have been stranded in a carriage accident. One discovers Ada's crypt and, in an attempt to remove the demon mask, cuts his hand. The blood drips onto Ada's corpse, stirring her revival and renewing her quest for human blood. In the meantime, the other traveler meets Ada's great-granddaughter, Princess Katia, also played by Steele. Ada's desire for a new life leads her to confront Katia in the hopes of gaining possession of her body. The confrontation is the traditional conflict between good and evil, but also sets mother (or in this case, great-grandmother) against daughter. Ada, like the witches of the *Malleus Maleficarum*, will devour her own to ensure her survival.

The sixties introduced Vampirella, an all-new female comic book character. Inspired by the movie, based on the French comic book character Barbarella, Forrest J Ackerman developed the character and wrote the introductory issue of this adult comic book. Vampirella hailed from Draculon, a vampire planet in which the rivers run with blood, not water. Vampirella is the only survivor of an environmental disaster which destroyed her planet. She arrives on Earth and finds that here blood runs only in living veins. Having no desire to kill, she learns to rely on a blood substitute for sustenance. Only when desperate does she turn to its

Vampirella, the sexy vampire with a heart of gold. (Photo courtesy of Forrest J Ackerman.)

human equivalent. She never kills without reason, and always mourns having to take human life. *Vampirella* was the longest running vampire comic book of all time, published consistently from her first appearance in 1969 through the last issue of the series (#112) in 1983. Six Vampirella novels adapted from the comic book also appeared in the mid-seventies. In 1991, Harris Comics revived the Vampirella character, and in 1996, Vampirella appeared in her first feature-length television movie.

Vampirella's scantily-clad voluptuousness certainly contributed to the development of Elvira, the vampire-like persona of actress Cassandra Peterson. Elvira was created in 1981 when Peterson was hired as a horror movie hostess for Los Angeles television affiliate KHJ-TV. Elvira became the first person to appear on television live and in 3-D when nearly three million pairs of 3-D glasses were distributed for a showing of the movie *The Mad Magician* (1954). Her newly-found celebrity catapulted her into the national limelight, and her program, *Movie Macabre*, went into syndication. Her popularity grew, and in 1982 she was able to put together a Halloween-oriented comedy cabaret at Knott's Berry Farm that has since become an annual event. Her television show was nominated for an Emmy. In 1985, she began to appear on *Thriller Theater*, a series of old B-movies re-released on video. She became the first female celebrity to endorse a beer product when she was hired by Coors in 1987, and has since started marketing her own microbrew called *Elvira's Night Brew*. Like Vampirella, she also appeared in a feature film, *Elvira: Mistress of the Dark* (1988), which told Elvira's life story. Descended from a line of sorcerers, Elvira's mother seeks to break out of the family tradition of witchcraft by marrying a mortal. Elvira is the result of the union. Part vamp and part valley girl, Elvira was the epitome of camp. Although the film was only a partial success in the theaters (the distributors, New World Pictures, went out of business soon after the film's release), it did quite well as a video release.

The eighties introduced a variety of new elements to the vampire formula. The growth of the home video market meant that films weren't measured solely by their success in the cinema houses. Movies that would otherwise have been considered industry flops found new life and new vigor as video releases. Other

Actress Cassandra Peterson drew from her real life experience as a Vegas showgirl in this scene from *Elvira: Mistress of the Dark* (1988). (Photo courtesy of Forrest J Ackerman.)

media influences such as MTV contributed to the genre as soundtracks featured more and more popular artists, occasionally with the artist herself in the role of the vampire (as in the case of Grace Jones as the erotic dancer and club owner in *Vamp*). This emphasis on youth was also reflected in the number of teenage protagonists in the vampire movies of the eighties, including *Fright Night* (1985), *Near Dark* (1987), and *The Lost Boys* (1987) and *Vamp* (1988). In *Vamp*, three college kids are in search of a stripper for their fraternity party when they stumble on Grace Jones and the other vampires of the After Dark Club.

A film that deviated from this teen vampire formula was Ken Russell's *Lair of the White Worm* (1988). Amanda Donahoe stars as Lady Arabella March, a devotee of the cult of the white worm, who feeds on human blood and makes virgin sacrifices to the colossal worm living in the caverns beneath her manor home. While director Ken Russell was able to camp up the story line, imbuing every element of the tale with sexual innuendo, it truly was not a far cry from the novel on which the film was based. Bram Stoker's last novel, *Lair of the White Worm* was written while he suffered from a dementia associated with Bright's disease. The over-the-top language and Freudian imagery probably could not have been handled in a less outrageous manner.

Grace Jones as Katrina performing at the After Dark Club in *Vamp* (1988). (Photo courtesy of Forrest J Ackerman).

But even as these new spectres came to the silver screen, there was another waiting in the wings. But first, the lesbian vampire.

Amanda Donahoe in snake form in *Lair of the White Worm* (1988). (Photo courtesy of Forrest J Ackerman.)

Ingrid Pitt as the vampire Carmilla in *Vampire Lovers* (1971).

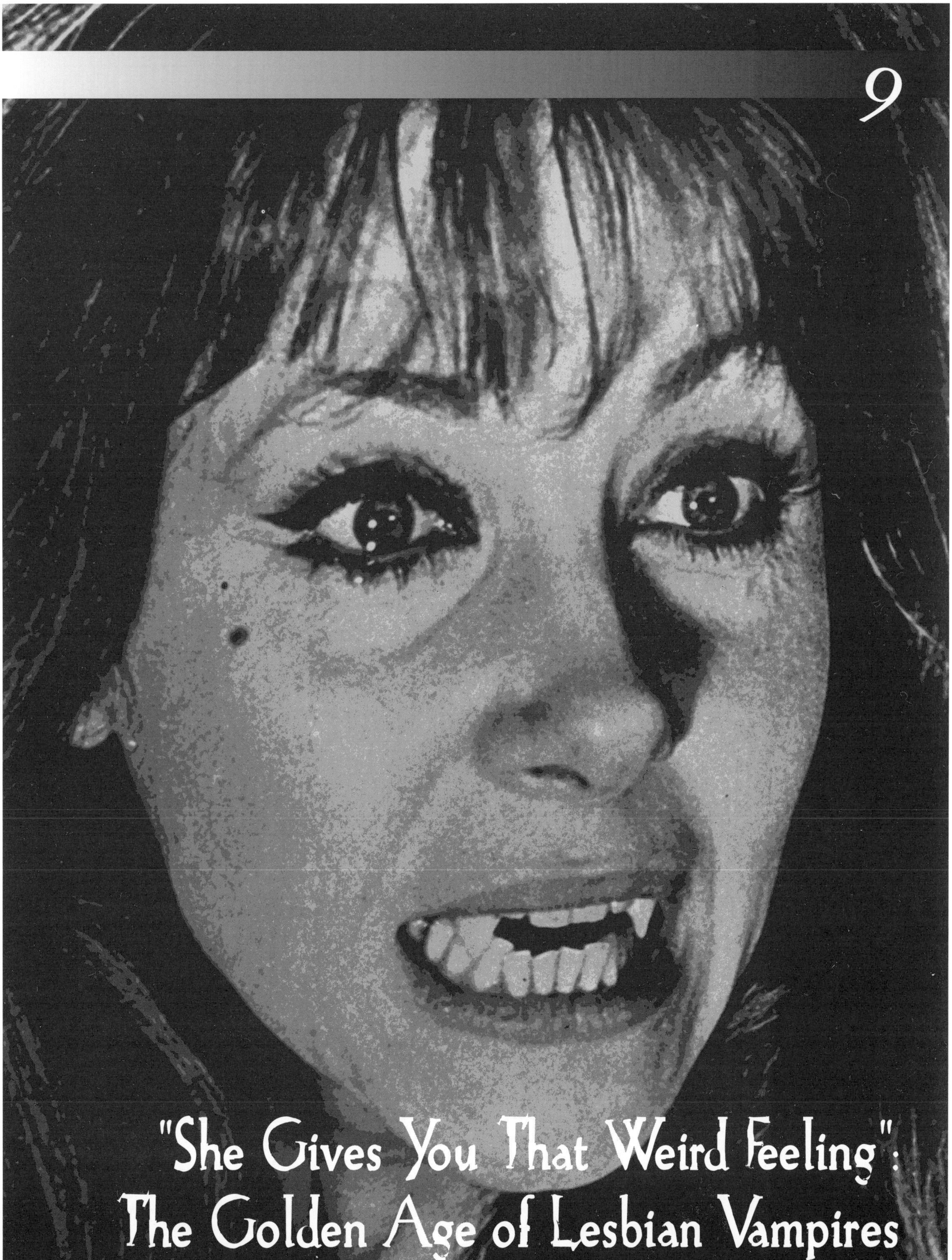

# 9

# "She Gives You That Weird Feeling": The Golden Age of Lesbian Vampires

Rarely are the twin themes of sex and death, and particularly death *through* sex, as sensationalized as in the lesbian vampire film. The highly sensual nature of vampire mythology, with its repeated references to "perversity" and "excessive" sexuality, provides a rich foundation for tales of lesbian desire. Coupling two archetypal social outlaws, the lesbian vampire film achieves a significance far beyond the easily-dismissed category of heterosexual male fantasy.

My first contact with the world of lesbian vampires was in 1983. I went to see *The Hunger* at a local theater. I really didn't know much about the film; I knew it was a vampire movie starring David Bowie. Imagine my surprise as I watched the cool, alluring, and sophisticated Catherine Deneuve seduce Susan Sarandon before my very eyes and on a very, very big screen. The two of them were making love in the most graphic and most erotic portrayal of lesbianism I had ever seen.

**...[T]he elegant and enigmatic Catherine Deneuve... playing an aristocratic vampire in Tony Scott's 1983 film *The Hunger*... swooped down on an innocent and utterly bedazzled Susan Sarandon and for eight hot minutes devoured her with explicit sex and unprecedented, everlasting sensual enthusiasm. Then she bit her, and the rest is history.**

– Judy Wieder, *The Advocate*

*The Hunger* certainly wasn't my first vampire movie. As a child, I loved watching the Saturday afternoon "Creature Feature." As a teenager, I stayed up until all hours to watch late-night vampire movies. In college, I dragged friends to out-of-the-way movie houses to see the occasional showing of old and/or foreign vampire films. By the time I saw *The Hunger*, I knew my interest in vampires was more than a passing phase. What I didn't know, sitting there in the dark with my boyfriend by my side, was that *he* was a passing phase, and that this Hollywood vampire movie would have much more of an impact on my future than I could, at that time, have possibly imagined. I suspect *The Hunger* had a similar effect on many nascent lesbians of my generation.

My own hunger kindled, the quest for lesbian vampire lore began. I discovered the spectre of the lesbian vampire rising time and time again—in the sadistic tales of Countess Bathory, the figure of Coleridge's Geraldine, the poetry of both Baudelaire and Swinburne, and LeFanu's Carmilla. Even among the earliest of vampire films, in *Vampyr* (1932) and *Dracula's Daughter* (1936), I found hints of this commanding and compelling creature. In cult horror films produced on the eve of the sexual revolution, I found overtly lesbian vampires wreaking havoc on the silver screen.

The popularity of the lesbian vampire in the late sixties and early seventies can be seen in the sheer number of vampire films with lesbian and female bisexual imagery during that time. Author and historian

Carmilla gently kisses Georgia while ensconsed in the greenhouse in *Blood and Roses* (1961).

Raymond McNally has referred to the years 1970–1974 as the "Golden Age of Lesbian Vampires." As many as twenty lesbian-themed vampire films were produced in that four-year period alone. Like the femme fatale before her, the lesbian vampire came to the forefront at a time of extreme social change. With the combined forces of the sexual liberation, women's and early gay movements, anxiety concerning sex and gender roles permeated much of popular culture. That fear of sexuality brings to mind the phobias of an earlier era, when the voracious sexual appetites of witches were described in the *Malleus Maleficarum*:

> [T]oward young girls, more given to bodily lusts and pleasures, witches observe a different method, working through their carnal desires and the pleasures of the flesh.

And it is through the pleasures of the flesh that the lesbian vampire lures her prey. The image of a lesbian vampire kissing a drop of blood from her victim's lips captivated audiences who went to see Roger Vadim's *Blood and Roses* (1961). A retelling of Sheridan LeFanu's "Carmilla," *Blood and Roses* was Roger Vadim's first vampire film. Vadim's was the first film treatment of "Carmilla" to exploit the story's homoeroticism.

Roger Vadim was a pioneer of sexually-explicit filmmaking and the art cinema of the fifties. Vadim's aesthetic was far more sexually-explicit than had previously been allowed in mainstream cinema, although his

Carmilla, in an intimate scene with the object of her desire, Emma, in *Vampire Lovers*. (1970)

style, talents and sensibilities transcended what was been thought of as pornography at that time. By challenging rigid censorship codes, Vadim's work not only paved the way for sexually-explicit filmmaking in France, but began to topple the dominos of film censorship throughout Europe and eventually in the United States as well.

Vadim made his mark with *And God Created Woman* (1956), starring his first wife, Brigitte Bardot. Although tame by contemporary standards, the film's sexual themes were remarkable at the time. *And God Created Woman* introduced Bardot as the French blonde bombshell, Bardot's claim to fame.

Vadim liked to feature his wives (or current lovers) in his movies. "Throughout his career," writes J. Gordon Melton in *The Vampire Book: The Encyclopedia of the Undead*, "Vadim searched for stories that would allow him to project his own sexual fantasies on the screen, and when he encountered the artistic presentation of an overtly sexual vampire...he was quick to see its potential." LeFanu's "Carmilla" was a perfect vehicle for Vadim and for his new wife, Annette Stroyberg (now known as Annette Vadim).

In *Blood and Roses*, Vadim updated the story of Carmilla, transporting her from the castles of her native Styria to a rural manor in modern France. In Vadim's retelling, Carmilla has been reincarnated and continues her search for her long lost love, her cousin Frédéric. He is engaged to another young woman, Georgia, whom Carmilla vengefully pursues throughout the film. In a scene where Carmilla and Georgia seek refuge from a rainstorm, Georgia pricks her finger on a rose thorn. It is when Georgia licks her wounded finger, leaving a drop of blood on her lips, that Carmilla leans forward and gently kisses the blood away.

Vadim went on to feature his next lover, Jane Fonda (they never married), in a film adaptation of a French comic book called Barbarella (1968). Vadim's contributions to the vampire genre can be said to include not only *Blood and Roses*, but also *Barbarella*, which later became the inspiration for Forrest J Ackerman's *Vampirella*.

Carmilla returned soon after in Thomas Miller's *Terror in the Crypt* (1963). Christopher Lee starred as Ludwig Karnstein, who fears that his daughter is the reincarnation of a witch. The vampiric witch is, in fact, his daughter's new friend, Lyuba. Lyuba's attachment to Karnstein's daughter builds with a slow and premeditated seduction in which the daughter becomes weaker and weaker as Lyuba becomes stronger. The lesbian subtext is barely visible, but the tale still does lend itself to an alternative reading. As the daughter loses herself in dreams, she and Lyuba run together through the castle grounds, with Lyuba representing freedom as much as she represents the daughter's eventual death.

## "Christopher Lee, in drag, in the Hammer films...is my ideal lesbian."

– Bertha Harris, "What Is a Lesbian?" quoted in Andrea Weiss' *Vampires and Violets: Lesbians in the Cinema*

It was another French filmmaker, Jean Rollin, who would pick up the threads of these tales and present truly graphic images of lesbian sexuality in his vampire films. Rollin's series of films—including *Queen of the Vampires* (1967), *Rape of the Vampires* (1967), *The Nude Vampire* (1969), *Thrill of the Vampire* (1970), *Requiem for a Vampire* (1971), and *Fascination* (1979)—all relied heavily on lesbian content. Emphasizing style over substance and sex over story line, the films of Jean Rollin achieved notoriety as soft-core porn classics with arresting visual imagery. In *Queen of the Vampires*, Rollin's first film, the vampire queen appears in black leather with whips and chains, the sado-masochistic empress of a harem of vampire women. In *Thrill of the Vampire*, a newly-wed couple is seduced by the vampire Isolde, who at one point emerges not from a coffin, but from the grandfather clock in the young bride's bedroom. Despite the frequently incoherent story lines, Rollin established an overt sexuality never before seen in vampire films. He has continued to do so with films such as *La Morte Vivante* (1982) and *The Two Vampire Orphans* (1995).

Spanish director Jesus Franco began his film career with *Bram Stoker's Dracula* (1970), an attempt at a faithful rendering of Stoker's novel. He went on to become famous for his adult erotic vampire movies. Unlike Jean Rollin, however, Franco was more interested in classic vampire stories. In *Vampyros Lesbos* (1970), Franco combines elements of the stories of Countess Bathory, Carmilla and Stoker's "Dracula's Guest." Like Rollin, Franco updates his story, opting for a modern setting and using an experimental jazz soundtrack that has found a renewed popularity as a compact disc. In *Vampyros Lesbos*, the heroine becomes infatuated with a descendent of Count Dracula, Nadine, who lures her to a remote island where she has already seduced a number of other victims. In a contempory tribute to Countess Bathory, Franco has Nadine kill her victims in order to maintain her youth. Other Franco films, including *Dracula's Daughter* (1972) and *Bare-Breasted Countess* (1973), marked a return to the baroque imagery of *Bram Stoker's Dracula* and visual treatment more in the style of Hammer films.

"Early in my teens, along with my best friend...I was seduced by a beautiful vampire who went by the name Carmilla....This vampire fed our growing curiosity about our bodies and presented us with the beginnings of a shared fantasy in whose arms we could begin to explore our sexualities...as a result my fantasy life has been imbued by the icon of the 'Hammer Horror' female vampire...she needs my fantasy to keep her from the patriarchal stake."

– Tanya Krzywinska, "La Belle Dame Sans Merci," in *A Queer Romance: Lesbians, Gay Men and Popular Culture* edited by Paul Burston and Colin Richardson.

Catherine Deneuve as Miriam in *The Hunger* (1983).

Hammer Studios, famous for their vampire movies since the late 1950s, turned their attention to Carmilla with *Vampire Lovers* (1970), the first film in Hammer's Karnstein Trilogy. Released for the 1971 centennial of publication of LeFanu's "Carmilla," *Vampire Lovers* featured Ingrid Pitt, who later portrayed the Countess Bathory in the Hammer Studios production of *Countess Dracula.* Unlike LeFanu's protagonist, Pitt is a rather voluptuous Carmilla (*The Vampire Book* calls her "amply endowed"), a far cry from the languid Carmilla of LeFanu's story. In *Vampire Lovers,* Carmilla pursues her prey under the guise of friendship, using her sensuality and physical appeal to lull her victim into a sense of security. When feeding, Carmilla gently strokes her young victim's breasts, inducing a near hypnotic state, before she finally bites. While other films of the genre relied on graphic depictions of violence, with much blood and gore, *Vampire Lovers* was more concerned with the sensual thrill of seduction.

The two other films in the Karnstein Trilogy deviated from the original Carmilla story line, while still relying on lesbian imagery to entertain and titillate. *Lust for a Vampire* (1970) was set in an all-girls' boarding school, and *Twins of Evil* (1971) starred Madeleine and Mary Collinson, *Playboy's* first Playmate twins.

The vampire films of the 1970s contained messages more subversive than simply their soft-core veneer would suggest. In *Blood Splattered Bride* (1972), a newlywed couple returns to the family estate to begin married life. The wife discovers her husband's genteel manner hides his hostility towards women, especially towards her. While exploring the basement, she discovers a faceless portrait her husband tells her is Mircalla Karnstein, a woman who murdered her husband on their wedding night. Karnstein, she learns, was discovered splattered with her husband's blood, having killed him when he forced her to perform "unspeakable acts." Mircalla appears in the wife's dreams, encouraging her to do away with her husband. When Mircalla appears in the flesh as the mysterious Carmilla, the wife's antipathy towards her husband increases. An exploration of female friendship, lesbian desire, and a damning critique of patriarchy and the institution of marriage follow. Upon learning the "true" nature of his wife's attachment to Carmilla, the husband kills both as they lie side by side in a coffin made for two.

Andrea Rau as Ilona, Countess Bathory's companion, in *Daughters of Darkness* (1971).

...the daughters of darkness are, in the old phrase, creatures of the night, ruled by the moon..., the female planet/goddess, both virginal and witchlike, who presides over all the feminine mysteries and cycles and controls the tides of blood and the sea.

– Carol Jenks, "Daughters of Darkness: A Lesbian Vampire Art Film" in *Necronomicon: Book One*

The Countess Bathory and Valerie share a quiet moment in *Daughters of Darkness* (1971).

D*aughters of Darkness* (1971) similarly subverts heterosexuality and the institution of marriage. The elements of sadism, hostility, and female subversion in this film are exaggerated even more than in *Blood Splattered Bride*. *Daughters of Darkness* opens with a newlywed couple returning to England to meet the groom's "mother" who turns out to be an aging male homosexual transvestite. Along the way they stop at a Belgian hotel, where the only other guests are the elegant Countess Bathory (Delphine Seyrig) and her beautiful and subservient female companion. Sensing sadistic tendencies in the groom, the Countess regales the young man with the exploits of her "ancestor," the notorious Countess Bathory. He, of course, is already familiar with the story. After the young man attacks his new wife, first beating her with a belt and then raping her, the Countess offers succor and support, eventually seducing the young wife and killing the husband. Critic Bonnie Zimmerman suggests that the "negative aspects of the vampire stereotype are mitigated when the viewer is herself a lesbian and feminist." She describes *Daughters of Darkness* as depicting lesbianism as "attractive" and heterosexuality as "abnormal and ineffectual."

**Different examples [of the lesbian in fiction] written by both lesbians and nonlesbians [fix] upon the otherness of the lesbian, primarily in the shape of the glamorous and dangerous vampire.... In self-defense, if for no other reason, we claim alienation as superiority and specialness, and glorify the status of the [lesbian] outlaw... a creature of tooth and claw, of passion and purpose: unassimilable, awesome, dangerous, outrageous, different: distinguished.**

– Bonnie Zimmerman, *The Safe Sea of Women: Lesbian Fiction 1969-1989*

Perhaps the only lesbian vampire film directed by a woman during this period is Stephanie Rothman's *Velvet Vampire* (1971). Rothman co-produced with legendary horror filmmaker Roger Corman throughout the 1960s and shares credit on a number of his productions. *Velvet Vampire* was her first foray into directing. The film features a distinct feminist subtext. In the opening sequence in downtown Los Angeles, the vampire thwarts an attempted rape. There are also several in-jokes linking Rothman's tale to the wider genre, including a vampire named Diana LeFanu (Celeste Yarnell) who is the proprietor of the Stoker Gallery. At the same time, Rothman turns the usual vampire clichés upside down. Rothman's vampire adores plants and sunlight and lives in the desert.

When a young couple breaks down in the desert, Rothman's LeFanu invites them to her home, where she wines and dines them. Gradually she seduces both the man and the woman. The woman, distraught over the horror she has witnessed, makes her escape. The final chase of vampire and her victim is unique, taking place not in dark rooms of a gothic manor or the wilds of the woods, but in the urban jungle of Los Angeles.

*Vampyres* (1974) marked a turning point for lesbian vampire films and the end of the Golden Age of Lesbian Vampires. Having presented explicit sex between women on the screen, the genre turned to graphic violence. *Vampyres* reveled in blood. While the groundwork had been laid by each of the lesbian vampire films

Fran and Miriam returning to the castle at the break of dawn in *Vampyres* (1974). (Photo courtesy of Forrest J Ackerman.)

previously mentioned, the blood in *Vampyres* flowed more profusely than ever, with the vampire lovers delectably licking and lapping the blood not only from the source, but from each other's bodies as well.

The coolly sensual vampire portrayed in *Daughters of Darkness* returned to the screen a decade later in *The Hunger* (1983). Adapted from a novel by Whitley Streiber, *The Hunger* is the story of Miriam (Catherine Deneuve), who calls to mind Delphine Seyrig's Countess Bathory in *Daughters of Darkness.* After two hundred years of agelessness, Miriam's companion, John (David Bowie), has begun to deteriorate at a rapid rate. John turns for help to Sarah (Susan Sarandon), a doctor researching the aging process. But it is too late for John, whose fate is clear. Miriam, afraid of being left alone, pursues Sarah. The resulting seduction has made *The Hunger* a cult classic of lesbian cinema. *The Hunger* and *Daughters of Darkness* joined the classic vampire to the classic femme fatale. Deneuve and Seyrig produced elegant monsters in the tradition of Dietrich and Garbo.

Like Baudelaire's Black Venus or Swinburne's Cleopatra, Deneuve's Miriam embodies the dual forces of life and death. She represents love and the pleasures love brings, but she is also a corrupting force, death beneath the face of beauty. She

Catherine Deneuve as Miriam and Susan Sarandon as Sarah in *The Hunger* (1983).

transmits the disease that is John's wasting sickness—the equivalent of the epidemics of the Middle Ages, tuberculosis in the eighteenth century, and syphilis in the nineteenth. In the late twentieth century, John's fate—the tragedy of his illness and his inability to stop the course of the disease—becomes an apt and powerful allegory for fear and desire in the time of AIDS, regardless of the film's intentions. "To the conscious mind," writes vampire historian and cultural critic David Skal, "the reality of AIDS can be almost too much to bear, but on the plane of fantasy, the threat of AIDS can be bargained with." AIDS underscores the intricate and often subtle intermingling of sex and death. Blood in vampire folklore brings this connection into even sharper focus. The vampire as a symbol of both deadly and erotic impulses highlights contemporary anxieties surrounding sex. Sexuality unleashed threatens the permanence of the status quo, but now the threat is no longer limited to the social framework—a threat to morality and culture. In reality, the bogey is not a vampire, but a virus, transmitted not by the supernatural, but by ordinary mortals. The dread and desire embodied by Miriam in *The Hunger* capture contemporary "real life" concerns and kindled renewed interest in the femme fatale.

Susan Sarandon wearing the ankh that symbolizes her transformation into a vampire in *The Hunger* (1983).

Sharon Stone as Catherine Trammel in *Basic Instinct* (1992).

10

# That's No Lady, That's Sharon Stone

In April of 1991, a copy of the working script for a sex thriller called *Basic Instinct* was leaked to Queer Nation, a gay activist organization known for guerrilla-style protests. Within weeks, Queer Nation members were on the scene of the film shoot in San Francisco, protesting what they saw as one more example

The smoldering eyes of the classic femme fatale.

of Hollywood perpetuating stereotypes of "killer" lesbians. The protests took a variety of forms. On-location civil disobedience included shouting, picketing, and paint-bombing the set. Some of the protesters presented script changes to the crew. One protester suggested replacing Michael Douglas with Kathleen Turner as a lesbian detective; others suggested that the script be amended so that women were victims of murder as well as men. Hoping to discourage people from seeing the film, protesters gave away the ending, going so far as to name one of their committees "Catherine Did It."

**You are dealing with a Sex Babe who could possibly be the Devil....If she is the Devil, Hell has improved.**

– *Rolling Stone* on Sharon Stone

The central character of *Basic Instinct* is Catherine Trammel (Sharon Stone), a bisexual mystery writer suspected of having murdered her rock star boyfriend, Johnny Boz, with an ice pick. The detective assigned to the case, Nick Curran (Michael Douglas), has just returned to work after a suspension resulting from his alcoholism and drug abuse. Police psychiatrist Beth Gardner, Curran's lover as well as his psychiatrist, is brought in when it is discovered that the method of Boz's murder was lifted from one of Trammel's novels. The plot becomes even more entangled when Curran is seduced by Catherine's icy, sensual demeanor. Everyone is a suspect, including Catherine's lesbian lover, Roxy, and Curran's psychiatrist who, we find out, had an affair with Trammel when they were in college.

While the plot turns on the investigation of Boz's murder, the movie is remembered for its sexual content, beginning with the opening scene of Boz tied to the bed frame while a woman's torso writhes above him (her identity is hidden by the movie's frame, her body shown from the neck down). Trammel's sexual prowess is noted time and time again. At one point, Curran refers to Trammel as "the fuck of the century." For Trammel, sex is a game. She toys with the male libido as easily and as shamelessly as a cat toys with a mouse before devouring her prey.

**"For me, a cute dyke with two Ferraris who kills men is a positive image."**

– Claire Beaven, Channel 4's Out series

Offended by the portrayal of homosexuals in *Basic Instinct*, Queer Nation orchestrated a nationwide media campaign calling attention to the sensationalized stereotyping of lesbian, gay and bisexual killers in Hollywood movies. What they failed to note was that the film's heterosexuals were equally offensive. At the same time, the activists heightened the visibility of a film that would become one of the largest grossing thrillers in movie history. The media campaign, launched a full year before the actual release of the film, contested the sex and violence that would become the chief selling point of an otherwise mediocre exploitation film.

# "Do you have any favorite contemporary actresses?" "I really admired Sharon Stone for her performance in *Basic Instinct.* That took guts."

– Betty Page, quoted in "An Exclusive Interview with Betty Page" by Bob Schultz in *Outre': The World of Ultra Media.*

Sharon Stone as Catherine Trammel with Leilani Sarelle Ferrer as her lover, Roxy, in *Basic Instinct* (1992).

When asked about the flap over *Basic Instinct*, Stone insisted on her support for Queer Nation's efforts. "This was a unique opportunity for the gay community to use a big media event to be heard....I'm enormously sympathetic with the issue that was raised."

Of course, Hollywood learned early on that publicity, even negative publicity, could persuade the public to flock to a film, even if only to see what all the fuss was about. More than eighty years before *Basic Instinct*, in March of 1918, the Women's Club of Omaha held a meeting to address the danger posed by Theda Bara's latest film, *Cleopatra*. Despite the historical topic, the Women's Club was appalled by the "wicked" and "suggestive" nature of the film, the shameful sensuality of its star, and the character's distinct lack of clothing. The Club's well-publicized condemnation of the film had one immediate result: an unprecedented demand for tickets to the film. The film sold out in Omaha and had similar success throughout the Midwest and the rest of the country. Theda Bara, the "Wickedest Woman in the World," had the last laugh once again.

Sharon Stone in a publicity shot from *The Quick and the Dead* (1995).

*Basic Instinct* was film number eighteen for Stone, whose list of B-movies read like a late-night cable line-up. Stone worked her way up through the ranks with films such as: *Allan Quartermaine and the Lost City of Gold* (1987), *Action Jackson* (1988), *Police Academy 4* (1986), and *He Said, She Said* (1991). Other A-list actresses—including Michelle Pfeiffer, Geena Davis, Julia Roberts, and Kim Basinger—didn't waste any time turning down the part of Catherine. For Stone, who has said that she was number fifteen on the list of actresses offered the part, it was a nothing-to-lose, everything-to-gain proposition. For the first time, she was playing a character who had sex appeal and a brain, too.

**...she projects a no-nonsense beauty—more sex subject than sex object.**

– Brian D. Johnson in *Maclean's*

It's Catherine's brain and her cool, calculating demeanor that gives *Basic Instinct* its suspenseful edge. Even so, the film will probably be remembered for its portrayal of another part of Stone's anatomy. In an interrogation scene, Stone's Catherine is center stage in a room full of lascivious detectives. While calmly answering their questions, she uncrosses then crosses her legs, meanwhile flashing the room with her obvious lack of *sous-vêtements*, causing the detectives to break out in an uncontrolled sweat. Bill Zehme, writing for *Rolling Stone*, describes the scene as having "quietly upstaged all other erotic histrionics in the movie." What makes Catherine Trammel so intriguing is her ability to be in control. The same can be said for Sharon Stone herself.

"Odysseus, when he was sleeping with the witch Circe,... always had the sword between him and her. I think that's the way to handle Sharon: have the knife ready."

– Joe Eszterhas on Sharon Stone

"He cannot abide that he adores me....It drives him fucking crazy! Oh, he adores me, the fool!"

– Sharon Stone on Joe Eszterhas

"This is what endears her to those straight and gay women in the audience who can tell a good thing in a bad film when they see it," writes *Sight and Sound's* Lizzie Francke. Her cool, manipulative eroticism in *Basic Instinct* catapulted Sharon Stone from the ranks of the B-movie queen to stardom.

Stone's first movie role was a bit part, "the pretty girl on the train" in Woody Allen's *Stardust Memories* (1980). From *Stardust Memories*, she went on to such films as Wes Craven's *Deadly Blessing* (1981), *The Vegas Strip Wars* (1984), and *King Solomon's Mines* (1985), playing parts she later described as Barbie roles. But with her role in *Basic Instinct*, Sharon Stone's performance became a standard by which other actresses would be measured. A standard for racy, steamy performances, but a standard nonetheless. Her Barbie doll image was a thing of the past; Stone had made it as a sultry sex goddess.

Like Theda Bara, Sharon Stone has had to fight to get roles that stretch her ability and showcase her acting. In the thriller *Intersection* (1994) with Richard Gere and Lolita Davidovich, Stone fought for and eventually got the role of the good wife after having been offered the role of the mistress. In *The Quick and the Dead* (1995), Stone not only stepped outside of the traditional femme fatale role, she also played a female lead who does not fall in love, get married, or take care of any one else's children—without a doubt a rare exception among films with female roles. *The Quick and the Dead* also marked Sharon Stone's first time as a film's producer.

But it was her performance in *Casino* (1995) that established her as a leading actress in a dramatic role. Directed by Martin Scorsese, *Casino* is set in Las Vegas in the early seventies. Sam "Ace" Rothstein (Robert De Niro) has come up through the ranks in the Midwestern mob and has been picked by the bosses to front their operation in Vegas. Ace runs his casinos with an iron hand, keeping the money rolling in and

Sharon Stone as Catherine Trammel resembling Catherine Deneuve's character in *The Hunger* (1983).

looking the other way as the "skim" (the mob's take) goes out. But his control starts to slip when he meets Ginger. The chip-hustling Ginger captivates Ace, and they eventually marry. Ace is in love, but for Ginger, it's the baubles that keep her captivated. As time goes on, the baubles mean less and less, and Ginger loses herself in drugs and alcohol.

**If you have a vagina and a point of view, that's a deadly combination.**

– Sharon Stone

The story of the beautiful grifter Ginger brought Stone not only a sought-after prestige role with an all-star cast, it also resulted in an Academy Award nomination for Best Supporting Actress. Her tremendous performance and well-deserved accolades came at a cost. Stone had to play a character gutted of all power before the critics took her seriously. Her best role to date was as a woman trapped, an alcoholic and a junkie whose choices in life were about having no choices at all. Ginger was a survivor, but only to a point

Sharon Stone shines as the predator. She is the Theda Bara for the nineties. Like Theda Bara, Sharon Stone is a small-town girl who made it big playing the woman you love to hate. Each studied their favorite performers. While Theda Bara spent most of her free time at the local movie theater, Sharon Stone watched old movies on television. Stone was fascinated with old movies and designed elaborate rituals to make watching them seem even more romantic: "There would be a fire going in the fireplace. I'd make myself a tray of Ritz crackers and cheese and lay it all out beautifully so that I could have this big, elaborate experience of watching movies—particularly Fred Astaire and Ginger Rogers movies."

**"Joan Crawford said she felt you were the only actress to have the talent, class, and courage to make it as a real star. Is there anyone you could say that about?"**

**"Yeah, Sharon Stone. She has style and determination, and there's no phoniness about her. She was very gutsy and courageous in *Basic Instinct.* She took a shot and she went for it. I think we're a lot alike."**

– Idol Chatter" with Faye Dunaway

Both women discovered a passion for performance as children. While Theda Bara performed in neighborhood barns, Sharon Stone was putting on elaborate plays in her family's double garage. Both went to New York to pursue their careers. Stone left her home in Meadville, Pennsylvania at seventeen to pursue a modeling career in New York; within days of her arrival, she was offered a contract with the Eileen Ford agency. Both landed life-changing and career-defining roles as women as dangerous as they are beautiful and alluring. *Basic Instinct* propelled Stone into the limelight, just as *A Fool There Was* would be Theda Bara's star vehicle. Unlike Theda Bara, who had William Fox and the entire studio system at work creating her image, Stone had to rely on her own skills, instincts, and opportunities to garner media attention. When the spotlight turned to Sharon Stone, she was ready to make the most of it.

Stone is, after all, a diva among divas, heir to a film tradition that includes the some of the greatest names of them all: Bette Davis, Joan Crawford, Gloria Swanson, Kim Novak, and Catherine Deneuve, just to name a few.

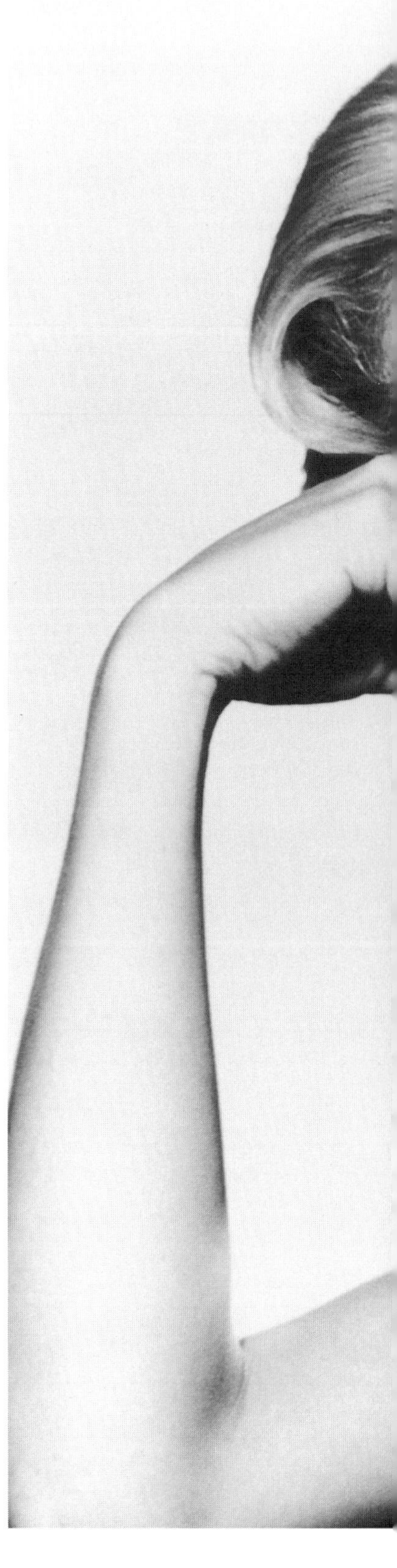

Sharon Stone is often credited with bringing back the glamour of Hollywood's "classic" era.

Catherine Trammel faces a room full of lecherous detectives in the interrogation room in *Basic Instinct* (1992).

We might not remember Sharon Stone for her artistry before the camera as much as for her powerful public persona. Even women we now remember as great actresses, in particular Bette Davis and Joan Crawford, had lean years, had to battle for even moderately challenging roles, and starred in a number of B-movie thrillers. Kim Novak, Gloria Swanson, and Greta Garbo left Hollywood all together when decent roles failed to materialize. At times, it seems we remember these actresses despite some of the roles they played. What Stone has in common with these women, and what has earned her a place in the annals of Hollywood history, is her incredible star power.

Stone has been credited with bringing old-fashioned glamour back to Hollywood. On heavy press days, she's been known to change outfits between each interview and each photo session, a practice nearly unheard of since the days of Joan Crawford and Norma Shearer. It's clear that she thoroughly enjoys her hard-won stardom and has learned to manipulate her public image in such a way that heightens her presence rather than diminishes it. Rather than abdicating the public realm, Stone basks in it. Every appearance is a performance. She is not simply the roles she plays on screen, but the larger-than-life image that she has created off-screen, and her greatest role to date is as Sharon Stone, Movie Star.

"Stardom is a reciprocal act of faith," writes journalist John Lahr in a column about Sharon Stone, "in which the star's duty is to make abundance incarnate and the audience's duty is to keep believing in the star's image." It's a duty that Stone relishes. "I think that when you get to be a famous person, there is a truth in the old-fashioned saying that, 'You belong to your public.' Your life and your creation belong to your public. What becomes your choice is what you embody. You can do or be anything you want."

**We're tired of being good all the time. When you deprive women of any notion of threat, it pretty much puts them back in the Victorian age. All innocent without power, except the power of being good.**

– Margaret Atwood

The reciprocity between the star and the audience is aided and abetted by the reciprocity between the star and the media. In much the same manner that Theda Bara's vampish "exoticism" was embraced by a burgeoning Hollywood media, Sharon Stone has become a favorite celebrity interviewee. In interviews, Sharon Stone, Predator, takes the stage. An *Esquire* headline reads: "Are You Man Enough for This Woman?" The interviewer, hopefully with tongue firmly in cheek, comments "Unsurprisingly, she is a carnivore, a woman who likes chewing flesh....Men fear her, and justifiably so. She is feral and forthright, quick and cunning." Meanwhile, magazine covers flash snappy teasers: "Surrender to Sharon Stone," "Sharon Stone Wants It All," and "Sharon Stone Shows Her Basic Instincts." Stone is portrayed as the ultimate Bitch Goddess, the woman to whom all men succumb and all women aspire. As Sharon Stone, Femme Fatale, she transcends even stardom and is propelled into the role of cultural icon. As Sharon Stone, Idol, she expands our notions of appropriate female behavior. There is the hint of daring, the thrill of the chase, the element of danger in everything she says and everything she does. When we embrace the media image of Sharon Stone, we get to drop the good girl role with which so many of us have been raised. She embodies women's desire to be bad.

Of course, there is another side to Sharon Stone. Like Crawford and Davis before her, Stone has demonstrated incredible fortitude, pursuing her goals with an unrelenting drive. Balancing her single-mindedness is her humor, her openness, her intelligence and her propensity for self-parody. Her commitment to AIDS awareness and to the American Foundation for AIDS Research (AMFAR) add another dimension to the off-

AMFAR spokesperson, Sharon Stone in *Diabolique* (1996)

screen Sharon Stone. Channeling her talents, skills, and media appeal, Stone has brought new life and new attention to AMFAR's efforts and goals. Like Elizabeth Taylor, in whose footsteps Stone has followed in her role as AMFAR spokesperson, Stone's celebrity will not rise and fall with the success or failure of her films. Sharon Stone is here to stay.

*Playboy*: Did acting brazenly and manipulatively in *Basic Instinct* affect your personality?

*Stone*: I'll tell you how it changed me. I received a fan letter from a woman who said "Thank you for your performance. I will never be a victim again." It did that for me, too.

– *Playboy*, December 1992

Glenn Close in *Fatal Attraction* (1987).

# 11

# Vamps and Vampires: The Nineties and Beyond

Our appetite for entertainment exploring the dark side of human nature is growing. Vamps and vampires share the limelight like never before. The Gothic subculture, a movement characterized by a vampiric aesthetic and a post-punk musical style that borrows its themes from classic horror, are the inheritors of the Romantic tradition, a vision of the world that celebrates death and decay. Vampires today, like the vampires of Keats, Shelley, and Baudelaire before them, are celebrated as romantic heroes, erotic icons of death and destruction.

Anne Parillaud as the vampire Marie in *Innocent Blood* (1992).

The femme fatale, too, is more popular than ever. Sexual politics have given way to frank sexual display, and the fetish wear associated with sexual perversion—cat suits, corsets, stilettos and riding crops, for example—are now considered "fetish fashion." The desire to be fashionably evil–to look and play the part of the femme fatale—has reached a level of expression not seen since the 1890s.

Perhaps it is the anxiety of the age that heightens the need and whets the appetite. Although considerable breakthroughs have been made regarding the treatment of AIDS, people are still dying, and the disease is still spreading. Other diseases, too, plague us. Tuberculosis, a disease once thought wiped out, has made a comeback, while hepatitis has become one of the most communicable sexually-transmitted diseases.

Perhaps this hunger can be attributed to the millennium. Although millenarian movements have come and gone—their predictions for the end of the world as we know it come to naught—there are still those who predict an apocalypse in the year 2000. The transition to a global economy and resulting extreme social and economic change has exacerbated the fears and tensions that support such apocalyptic visions of the future.

One thing is certain. The proliferation of independent film producers, cable movie programs, and straight-to-video productions means there is an ever-increasing flow of movies with which to feed our hunger.

While Sharon Stone was bearing it all for *Basic Instinct*, director Francis Ford Coppola was injecting new blood into the vampire genre with his forty million dollar production *Bram Stoker's Dracula* (1992). Although vampire movies were made throughout the 1980s and even into the 1990s, the level of mainstream attention paid to Coppola's *Dracula* was matched only by the screen adaptation of Anne Rice's *Interview with the Vampire* (1994).

**"[Lilith] is absolutely fabulous....She's strong, she's powerful, she's a woman in every sense of the word. She gets to be sexy and intelligent and love life and be happy and have fun. Just very happy to be alive."**

– Angie Everhart in *Fangoria* magazine on playing the vampire in *Bordello of Blood*

While female vampires have not garnered the blockbuster attention of either *Dracula* or *Interview*, they have been busy throughout the decade. Anne Parillaud, who played the elegant assassin in the French film *La Femme Nikita* (1990), made her American debut as Marie, a French vampire with a conscience, in *Innocent Blood* (1992). Mexican actress Salma Hayek appeared as the vampire stripper in Quentin Tarantino's genre spoof *From Dusk 'Til Dawn* (1994). Supermodel Angie Everhart made her contribution as Lilith, the vampire queen who is the madam of a vampire brothel in *Tales from the Crypt's Bordello of Blood* (1995). Independent and art cinema, too, has turned to the vampire for inspiration. In *Nadja* (1994), Dracula's daughter (Elina Lowensohn) wanders the streets of Manhattan's East Village bemoaning her fate and her abusive childhood. In *The Addiction* (1995), Lili Taylor plays Kathleen, a New York philosophy student whose ability to draw the line between good and evil crumbles when she herself becomes a vampire. The vampire woman challenges Kathleen to protect herself, demanding that Kathleen reject her. Kathleen's inability to assert herself, even when provoked to do so, seals her fate. Ironically, it is only as a vampire that Kathleen can come to terms with herself, her capacity for both good and evil, and, in the end, with her own inner power.

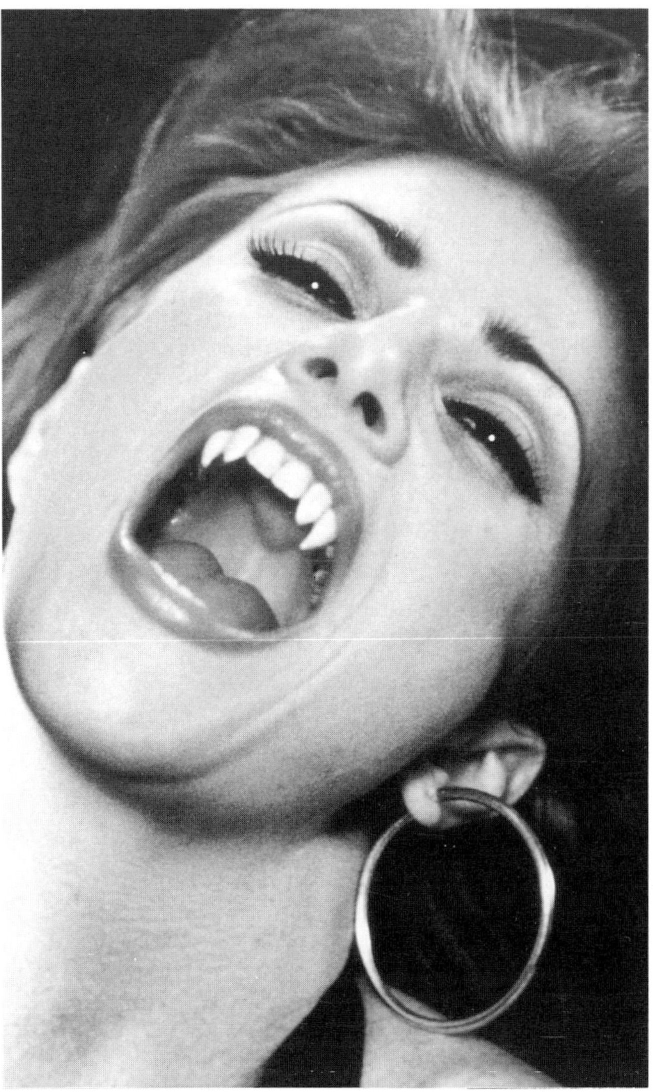

Lilith (Angie Everhart) shows her fangs before feasting in *Tales from the Crypt's Bordello of Blood.*

**Hayek may be sultry to the point of heat exhaustion, but she's also in on the cosmic joke....In an ironic age, she's our Salome.**

– Michael Atkinson, in *Interview*

Femmes fatales, too, have had a renaissance of sorts in the movies. The success of *Basic Instinct* generated an even wider array of femmes fatales, each one, it seems, more nasty than the one before. Michael Douglas, who went head-to-head with Glenn Close's psychotic, knife-wielding nymphomaniac in *Fatal Attraction* (1987), returned to the role of the beleaguered white male targeted by sexy, powerful women in *Disclosure* (1994). Joe Eszterhas, *Basic Instinct's* screenwriter, also returned to familiar territory with his script for the thriller *Jade* (1995). *Romeo Is Bleeding* is notable for Lena Olin's performance as Mona Demarkov, a hit woman who, among other sadistic acts, strangles her assailant by taking his neck between her muscular thighs.

Independent productions such as *Red Rock West* (1994) also received critical acclaim in the nineties. In *Red Rock West,* a young man (Nicholas Cage) is mistaken for a hit man hired to kill an adulterous wife (Lara Flynn Boyle). The wife offers the hit man twice as much to kill her husband instead. Director John Dahl followed the success of *Red Rock West,* his first film, with another femme fatale thriller. *The Last Seduction* (1994) stars Linda Fiorentino as Bridget, one of the most heartless femmes fatales to grace the screen in a long, long time. Bridget succeeds in seducing two men, bending them to her nefarious will, only to frame them both while she gets away with murder.

Salma Hayek as the erotic dancing vampire queen in *From Dusk 'Til Dawn.*

Gina Gershon as Corky and Jennifer Tilly as Violet in *Bound* (1996).

**For me, stealing has always been a lot like sex. The only difference is, I can fuck someone I just met. But to steal? I need to know someone like I know myself.**

– Corkey, in *Bound*

The sheer nastiness of these women, and the cold and calculating manner in which they destroy those around them, has already reached the point of cliché. Even now, a new femme fatale is making her way into the movies. In *Bound* (1996), Violet (Jennifer Tilly) is a mobster's wife who conspires with Corkey (Gina Gershon), a tough-talking butch lesbian who becomes her lover, to steal two million dollars that has been placed in her husband's care. While the women of films such as *Disclosure*, *Jade*, *Red Rock West* and *The Last Seduction* portray women as untrustworthy, the crux of the plot in *Bound* centers on the trust these two women place in each other. Violet is able to maneuver her sexuality around her immediate needs, pleasing her husband and flirting with the Mafiosos who are her husband's bosses. But when it comes to her own desires, Violet is far from the coy, sweet gangster's moll she appears to be. She is willing to use her body as a tool, but to trust someone with her life requires a different sort of intimacy.

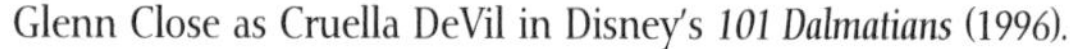

Glenn Close as Cruella DeVil in Disney's *101 Dalmatians* (1996).

Linda Fiorentino as Bridget in *The Last Seduction* (1994).

Maggie Cheng in *Irma Vep* (1997) offers another look at the new face of the femme fatale. Cheng plays herself in this French film about the remaking of an early serial telling the story of a group of jewel thieves called *Les Vampires*. Irma Vep (an anagram for "vampire") is the gang's leader, and Cheng is to recreate the original role. The director knows Cheng, an actress in Hong Kong action films, has the style and grace of a cat burglar, but her instinct is all wrong. "You've got to feel the part," he tells her. Cheng returns to her hotel, dressed in her latex cat suit, and pulls a heist within the very walls of her hotel. The jewels are worthless, costume jewelry laid aside by a woman who is on the phone fighting with her boyfriend even as Cheng prowls around the room completely unnoticed by her victim. The crime is dispassionate, the token necklace worthless. She just wants to know what it feels like to play the role.

As we look to the future, vampires and femmes fatales are as prodigious and prolific as their nineteenth-century counterparts a century ago. Like Cheng, we all want to know what it feels like to be bad.

Amanda Bearse as the girl-next-door gone bad in *Flight Night* (1985).

12

# In Praise of Wicked Women

**"[W]e had found a secret talisman against a nice girl's life. Vampires were supposed to menace women, but to me at least, they promised protection against a destiny of girdles, spike heels and approval."**

Salma Hayek in a publicity shot from *Desperado* (1995).

– Nina Auerbach, *Our Vampires, Ourselves*

Throughout history, women and men have been drawn to the femme fatale—as a figure of worship in the form of the Dark Goddess; as something dreaded and feared in the image of the witch; as the folkloric vampire whose bite brings both pleasure and pain; and, as the sensual and seductive predatory lover. What was once sacred has now entered the realm of popular culture. Yet even in her profane form, the femme fatale is worshipped, embodying our longing for power, our desire and fear.

The femme fatale, like the female vampire, is more than just a pop-culture figure. She is an icon, a symbol for women aspiring to independence, self-determination and erotic power. Many critics argue that this power—a destructive power limited to a sexual realm—reduces the femme fatale to just another sex symbol. The femme fatale certainly exists in the sexual realm, and much of her power is derived from the control she exerts over others using her seductive allure. But she also challenges the status quo. The femme fatale—the Goddess who devours her own children, the witch who sacrifices babies to the Devil, the mistress who is master of her own life, and the vampire for whom the rules of social engagement no longer apply—defies traditional social and patriarchal norms. She has rejected the traditional role of mother and wife and has embraced and celebrated her sexuality on her own terms. She has escaped or transcended all conventional forms of morality. And this is the key element that makes a woman fatal. She is the virgin in the oldest sense of the word—a woman unto herself, beyond definition and beyond control, dedicated to a higher purpose. She is also the whore, a woman who embraces and celebrates her sexuality at all costs.

The fatal woman is a sexual fantasy for both men and women. She is an image of both desire and fear; she both attracts and repels. She reaches out to the rebel in each of us. At the same time, she is vilified and hunted by those who cannot accept her or her ways. The story of the femme fatale, like the story of the vampire, more often than not ends in destruction: the femme fatale ruined when her deeds come back to haunt her, the vampire with a stake through her breast. But her spirit—the devouring mother, the predatory lover, the dark goddess, the outcast—lives on.

Louise Brooks

Woman is most dangerous when she disregards the expectations placed on her by others. Beyond the control of society, family, religion, and tradition, she is who she is without fear or regret. When a woman is a free agent, she is chastised, demonized, and damned. No longer simply De Beauvoir's Other, she is now the monster:

> In place of the myth of the laborious honeybee or the mother hen is the myth of the devouring female insect: the praying mantis, the spider. No longer is the female she who nurses the little ones, but rather she who eats the male; the egg is no longer a storehouse of abundance, but rather a trap of inert matter in which the spermatozoon is castrated and drowned. The womb, that warm, peaceful, and safe retreat, becomes a pulp of humors, a carnivorous plant, a dark contractive gulf, where dwells a serpent that insatiably swallows up the strength of the male. The same dialectic makes the erotic object into a wielder of black magic, the servant into a traitress, Cinderella into an ogress, and changes all women into enemies... (*The Second Sex*)

"...what happens to most of these men is that the tables are turned on them by women who turn out to be wiser than they thought."

– Danny Peary, *Cult Movies*

Gloria Swanson.

We are fascinated and amazed by these "enemy" women. Styles, fashions, and politics may change, but the wicked woman remains essentially the same. She is more than a stereotype. She is an archetype, a universal image. She is exhilarating and exciting, even as she performs deeds deemed evil and cruel. She is as much an icon as the Virgin Mary, although the femme fatale is an instrument for a different kind of faith. She is the image of woman's strength, autonomy, and desirability, the woman we love to hate. Icons, it is said, are an aid to worship, a tool for creating a sacred space. The femme fatale is a divinity of her own kind. She is the dark goddess. Through her we explore our own darkest places and our deepest desires. Through her we find our vengeance, our anger and our desire to be bad. Through her we live life on the edge and through her we find ways of expressing the most difficult and treacherous parts of ourselves.

Katherine Hepburn.

# Bibliography

# Bibliography


Allen, Virginia M. *The Femme Fatale: Erotic Icon.* New York: Whitston, 1983.

Apuleius. *The Golden Ass.* Translated by Jack Lindsay. Bloomington: Indiana University Press, 1960.

Atkinson, Michael. "Take a Hayek." *Interview.* February 1997, pp. 112–14.

Atwood, Margaret. "Zenia is sort of like Madonna." The *New York Times Book Review.* October 31, 1993, p. 93.

Auerbach, Nina. *Our Vampires, Ourselves.* Chicago: University of Chicago Press, 1995.

Bade, Patrick. *Femme Fatale: Images of Evil and Fascinating Women.* New York: Mayflower Books, 1979.

Barstow, Anne Llewellyn. *Witchcraze: A New History of the European Witch Hunts.* San Francisco: HarperCollins, 1995.

Beauvoir, Simone de. *The Second Sex.* New York: Vintage Books, 1952.

Berdan, Frances F. and Patricia Rieff Anawalt. *The Codex Mendoza.* Berkeley: University of California Press, 1992.

Bird, Daniel. "Fascination: Jean Rollin, Cinematic Poet," in *Necromonicon One,* edited by Andrew Black. London: Creation Books, 1996.

Blumenstock, Peter. "Jean Rollin Has Risen from the Grave," in *Video Watchdog.* No. 31, pp.36–57.

Bone, Eugenia. "If Looks Could Kill." *Harper's Bazaar.* October 1992, p.173.

Borland, Carroll. *Countess Dracula.* Absecon, NJ: Magicimage Books, 1994.

Brownlow, Kevin. *Hollywood: the Pioneers.* New York: Alfred A. Knopf, 1979.

Campbell, Virginia. "Sweet Charity," in *Movieline.* September 1996, pp.46–54, 94–95.

Carter, A. E. *Charles Baudelaire.* Boston: Twayne Publishers, 1977

Cavendish, Richard. *Man, Myth & Magic: The Illustrated Encyclopedia of Mythology, Religion and the Unknown.* New York: Marshall Cavendish, 1995.

"Censors on the Street." *Time.* May 13, 1991, p. 70.

Coleridge, Samuel Taylor. *The Rime of the Ancient Mariner and Other Poems.* New York: Penguin Books, 1995.

Comte, Michel. "Sharon's Back in Town." *Vanity Fair.* March 1996, pp.154–61, 196–98.

Conway, Michael and Mark Ricci. *The Films of Marilyn Monroe.* New York: Carol Publishing Group,1968.

Damon, Gene. "Lesbiana," in *The Ladder.* March 1971, p.36.

DeCaro, Frank. "Idol Worship," in *Out.* March 1997, pp. 68–75.

Edgren, Gretchen. *The Playmate Book: Five Decades of Centerfolds.* Santa Monica: General Publishing Group, 1996.

Eyles, Allen, Robert Adkinson and Nicholas Fry. *House of Horror: The Complete Hammer Films Story.* London: Andrew Sinclair Productions, Ltd., 1994.

Francke, Lizzie. "Someone to Look At", in *Sight and Sound.* March 1996, p.26.

Gandee, Charles. "Star Turn," in *Vogue.* December 1993, pp. 256–64, 328–29.

Genini, Ronald. *Theda Bara: A Biography of the Silent Screen Vamp, with a Filmography.* Jefferspon, NC: McFarland & Co., Inc., 1996.

George, Demetra. *Mysteries of the Dark Moon: The Healing Power of the Dark Goddess.* San Francisco: HarperCollins, 1992.

Golden, Eve. *Vamp: The Rise and Fall of Theda Bara.* New York: Emprise Publishing, Inc., 1996.

"Good Evening, I am Vampira," in *Life.* June 14, 1954, pp. 107–8, 110.

Graves, Robert. *The White Goddess.* New York: Farrar, Straus & Giroux, 1948.

Graves, Robert and Raphael Patai. *Hebrew Myths: The Book of Genesis.* New York: Greenwich House, 1983.

Guiley, Rosemary Ellen. *The Complete Vampire Companion: Legend and Lore of the Living Dead.* New York: Macmillan, 1994.

Hadleigh, Boze. *Bette Davis Speaks.* New York: Barricade Books, 1996.

Handelman, David. "Film Star Noir," in *Vogue.* May 1992, p.222.

Heller, Reinhold. *The Earthly Chimera and the Femme Fatale: Fear of Woman in Nineteenth Century Art.* Chicago: University of Chicago, 1981.

Higashi, Sumiko. *Virgins, Vamps, and Flappers: The American Silent Movie Heroine.* Montreal: Eden Press, 1978.

Hirschberg, Lynn. "Say It Ain't So, Joe," in *Vanity Fair.* August 1991, pp.76–85.

Hugo, Victor. *Notre-Dame de Paris.* New York: Oxford University Press, 1993.

Jacobs, Andrew. "Can She Make AIDS Hot Again?," in *New York.* April 8, 1996, pp.28-35.

Jefferson, Margo. "Woman as Icon: Disturbing, Inspiring," in the *New York Times.* December 10, 1996, p. C15.

Jenks, Carol. "Daughters of Darkness: A Lesbian Vampire Art Film," in *Necromonicon One,* edited by Andy Black. London: Creation Books, 1996.

*John Willie's Bizarre.* Taschen. Cologne, Germany. 1996.

Johnson, Brian D. "Killer Movies," in *Maclean's.* March 30, 1992, pp. 48-51.

Jones, Stephen. *The Illustrated Vampire Movie Guide.* London: Titan Books, 1993.

Kauffman, L.A. "Queer Guerrillas in Tinseltown," in *The Progressive.* July 1992, p. 36.

Keesey, Pam. *Personal Communication with Maila Nurmi at the Son of Famous Monsters Convention.* Hollywood, CA. May 27, 1995.

Keesey, Pam. "Introduction," in *Daughters of Darkness.* Pittsburgh, PA: Cleis Press, 1993.

—. "Introduction," in *Dark Angels.* Pittsburgh, PA: Cleis Press, 1995.

King, Teresa. *The Divine Mosaic: Women's Image of the Sacred Other.* St. Paul, MN: Yes International Publishers, 1994.

Kobal, John. *Rita Hayworth: The Time, the Place, the Woman.* New York: W.W. Norton, 1977.

Krzywinska, Tanya. "La Belle Dame Sans Merci," in *A Queer Romance: Lesbians, Gay Men & Popular Culture,* edited by Colin Richardson. London: Routledge,1995.

Lahr, John. "The Big Picture," in *The New Yorker.* March 25, 1996, pp.72-78.

Leaming, Barbara. *Bette Davis: A Biography.* New York: Ballantine, 1992.

Lee, Tanith. *Women as Demons.* London: The Women's Press, 1989.

Levy, Emanuel. "Vampira: About Sex, Death, and Taxes," in *Variety.* November 18, 1996, p. 63.

Loos, Anita. "The New Vamp," in *Jane Mulvagh's The Vogue History of Twentieth Century Fashion.* New York: Viking Penguin, 1989.

Lucas, Tim. "Versions and Vampires," in *Video Watchdog.* No. 31, pp.28-35.

Malkin, Marc S. "Idol Chatter," in *Premiere.* October 1996, p.34.

Maltin, Leonard. *Leonard Maltin's 1998 Movie & Video Guide.* New York: Signet, 1997.

Mandelbaum, Howard. "Bette Davis: A Talent for Hysteria," in *Bright Lights Film Journal.* #18. www.slip.net/~gmm/bright.html. www.page@url. version current@August 1997.

Marigny, Jean. *Vampires: Restless Creatures of the Night.* New York: Harry N. Abrams, 1994.

McNally, Raymond. *A Clutch of Vampires.* Greenwich, CT: New York Graphic Society, 1974.

—. *In Search of Dracula.* Greenwich, CT: New York Graphic Society, 1972.

Melton, J. Gordon. *The Vampire Book: The Encyclopedia of the Undead.* Detroit: Visible Ink, MI. 1994.

Morris, Gary. "Betty Boop," in *Bright Lights Film Journal.* #16. www.slip.net/~gmm/bright.html. www.page@url. version current@August 1997.

Murray, Raymond. *Images in the Dark: An Encyclopedia of Gay and Lesbian Film and Video.* Philadelphia: TLA Productions, 1994.

Newton, Steve. "The Best Little Bordello of Blood," in *Fangoria.* March 1996, pp.20-21.

Oates, Joyce Carol. " 'At Least I Have Made a Woman of Her': Images of Women in Twentieth-Century Literature," in *The Georgia Review.* Spring 1983, pp.7-30.

Pagels, Elaine. *The Origin of Satan.* New York: Random House, 1996.

Patai, Raphael. *The Hebrew Goddess.* New York: KTAV Publishing House, 1967.

Paz, Octavio. *The Bow and the Lyre.* Austin: University of Texas Press, 1973.

—. "Hieroglyphs of Desire," in *Nostalgia for Death.,* edited by Xavier Villaurrutia. Port Townsend, WA: Copper Canyon Press, 1993.

Peary, Danny. *Cult Movies: The Classics, the Sleepers, the Weird, and the Wonderful.* New York: Delta Books, 1981.

—. *Cult Movies 2: The Classics, the Sleepers, the Weird, and the Wonderful.* New York: Delta Books, 1983.

Penrose, Valentine. *The Bloody Countess: The Crimes of Erszebet Bathory.* London: Creation Books, 1970.

Picardie, Ruth. "Mad, Bad and Dangerous," in *New Statesman & Society.* May 1, 1992, p.36.

Praz, Mario. *The Romantic Agony.* New York: Oxford University Press, 1970.

Purkiss, Diane. *The Witch in History: Early Modern and Twentieth-Century Representations.* New York: Routledge, 1997.

Queen, Carol. "Fucking with Madonna," in *Real Live Nude Girl: Chronicles of Sex-Positive Culture.* San Francisco, Cleis Press, 1997.

Riede, David G. Swinburne: *A Study of Romantic Mythmaking.* Charlottesville: University Press of Virginia, 1978.

Robbins, Rossell Hope. *The Encyclopedia of Witchcraft and Demonology.* New York, Crown Publishers, Inc., 1959.

Rollyson, Carl E. Jr. *Marilyn Monroe: A Life of the Actress.* Ann Arbor: UMI Research Press, 1986.

Rosen, Marjorie. *Popcorn Venus: Women, Movies and the American Dream.* New York: Avon Books, 1973.

Salmonson, Jessica Amanda. *The Encyclopedia of Amazons: Women Warriors from Antiquity to the Modern Era.* New York: Paragon House, 1991.

Schultz, Bob. "An Exclusive Interview with Betty Page," in *Outré: The World of Ultra Media.* No. 3, pp. 42–46.

Schwartz, Howard. *Lilith's Cave.* New York: Harper & Row, 1988.

"Sharon Stone," in *Current Biography.* April 1996, pp. 52–55.

"Sharon Stone Shows Her Basic Instincts," in *Playboy.* December 1992, pp.63–88.

Sharrett, Christopher. "Hollywood Homophobia," in *USA Today Magazine.* July 1992, p.93.

Simpson, Janice C. "Out of the Celluloid Closet," in *Time.* April 6, 1992. p.65.

Sischy, Ingrid. "Wanted Alive!" *Interview.* February 1997, pp.84–89, 118–19.

Skal, David. *Hollywood Gothic: The Tangled Web of Dracula from Novel to Stage to Screen.* New York: W.W. Norton, 1990.

—. *The Monster Show: A Cultural History of Horror.* New York: W.W. Norton, 1993.

—. *V is for Vampire: The A-Z Guide to Everything Undead.* New York: Plume/Penguin, 1996.

Spada, James. *More Than a Woman: An Intimate Biography of Bette Davis.* New York, Bantam,1993.

Stein, Karen F. "Monsters and Madwomen: Changing Female Gothic," in *The Female Gothic,* edited by Juliann E. Fleener. Montreal: Eden Press, 1983.

Stephens, John Richard. *Vampires, Wine & Roses.* New York: Berkeley Books, 1997.

Stine, Whitney, with a running commentary by Bette Davis. *Mother Goddam: The Story of the Career of Bette Davis.* New York: Hawthorn Books, 1974.

Stone, Merlin. *When God Was a Woman.* San Diego: Harcourt, Brace, Jovanovich, 1976.

Sullivan, Jack. *The Penguin Encyclopedia of Horror and the Supernatural.* New York: Viking Penguin, 1986, pp. 375–77.

Summers, Montague. *The Malleus Maleficarum of Heinrich Kramer and James Sprenger.* New York: Dover Publications, 1971.

Thomas, Bob. *Joan Crawford.* New York: Simon & Schuster, 1978.

Twitchell, James B. "Frankenstein and the Anatomy of Horror," in *The Georgia Review.* Spring 1983, pp.41–78.

Ursini, James and Alain Silver. "The Female Vampire," in *The Vampire Film.* New Brunswick, NJ: A.S.Barnes & Co., 1975, pp.97–121.

Vogue Editors. *On the Edge: Images from One Hundred Years of Vogue.* New York: Random House, 1992.

Walker, Alexander. *Bette Davis: A Celebration.* Boston: Little, Brown & Co., 1986.

Walker, Barbara G. *The Woman's Encyclopedia of Myths and Secrets.* San Francisco: HarperCollins, 1983.

Weiss, Andrea. *Vampires and Violets: Lesbians in the Cinema.* London: Jonathan Cape, 1992.

Wieder, Judy. "Deneuve," in *The Advocate.* July 25, 1995, pp.50–55.

Winer, Laurie. "Death Becomes Him," in *Harper's Bazaar.* October 1992, pp.171–2.

Wolf, Leonard. *Dracula: The Connoisseur's Guide.* New York: Broadway Books, 1997.

—. *A Dream of Dracula: In Search of the Living Dead.* New York: Popular Library, 1972.

Zehme, Bill. "Are You Man Enough for This Woman?" in *Esquire.* March 1995, pp 84–91.

—. "Hot Cover." *Rolling Stone.* May 14, 1992, pp. 43–46, 118.

Zierold, Norman. *Sex Goddesses of the Silent Screen.* Chicago: Henry Regnery Co., 1973.

Marlene Dietrich in *The Song of Songs* (1933).

# Filmography & Videography

## Filmography

There are a variety of wonderful film and video reference books that will help you track down a vast array of interesting films. Every home should have one. Reference books that have been particular useful in researching this book are: *Videohound's Golden Movie Retriever 1997* (Visible Ink Press, Detroit, MI, 1997); *An Illustrated Vampire Movie Guide* edited by Stephen Jones (Titan Books. London, England, 1993); and *Images in the Dark* edited by Raymond (TLA Productions. Philadelphia, PA, 1994.)

The films you'll find listed here are among my favorites movies, examples of the femme fatale, classic cinema, or in some cases, cult favorites.

### Theda Bara

*Forty-Five Minutes from Hollywood* (1926)
*Madame Mystery* (1926)
*Unchastened Woman, The* (1925)
*Prince of Silence, The* (1921)
*Belle Russe, La* (1919)
*Kathleen Mavourneen* (1919)
*Light, The* (1919)
*Lure of Ambition, The* (1919)
*Siren's Song, A* (1919)
*When Men Desire* (1919)
*Woman There Was, A* (1919)
*Salome* (1918)
*Forbidden Path, The* (1918)
*She Devil, The* (1918)
*Soul of Buddha, The* (1918)
*Under the Yoke* (1918)
*When a Woman Sins* (1918)
*Cleopatra* (1917)
*Camille* (1917)
*Heart and Soul* (1917)
*Her Greatest Love* (1917)
*Tiger Woman, The* (1917)
*Darling of Paris, The* (1917)
*Madame Du Barry* (1917)
*Rose of Blood, The* (1917)
*Vixen, The* (1916)
*Romeo and Juliet* (1916)
*Her Double Life* (1916)
*Under Two Flags* (1916)
*Eternal Sappho, The* (1916)
*Serpent, The* (1916)
*East Lynne* (1916)
*Gold and the Woman* (1916)
*Destruction* (1915)
*Galley Slave, The* (1915)
*Carmen* (1915)
*Sin* (1915)
*Two Orphans, The* (1915)
*Lady Audley's Secret* (1915)
*Aka Secrets of Society* (1915)
*Devil's Daughter, The* (1915)
*Clemenceau Case, The* (1915)
*Fool There Was, A* (1915)
*Kreutzer Sonata, The* (1915)

### Joan Crawford

*Trog* (1970)
*Berserk* (1968)
*I Saw What You Did* (1965)
*Strait Jacket* (1964)
*Caretakers, The* (1963)
*Whatever Happened to Baby Jane?* (1962)
*Best of Everything, The* (1959)
*Story of Esther Costello, The* (1957)
*Autumn Leaves* (1956)
*Queen Bee* (1955)
*Female on the Beach* (1955)
*Johnny Guitar* (1954)
*Torch Song* (1953)
*Sudden Fear* (1952)
*This Woman Is Dangerous* (1952)
*Goodbye My Fancy* (1951)
*Harriet Craig* (1950)
*The Damned Don't Cry* (1950)
*It's a Great Feeling* (1949)
*Flamingo Road* (1949)
*Daisy Kenyon* (1947)
*Possessed* (1947)
*Humoresque* (1946)
*Mildred Pierce* (1945)
*Hollywood Canteen* (1944)
*Above Suspicion* (1943)
*They All Kissed the Bride* (1942)
*Reunion in France* (1942)
*When Ladies Meet* (1941)
*Woman's Face, A* (1941)
*Strange Cargo* (1940)
*Susan and God* (1940)
*Women, The* (1939)
*Ice Follies of 1939, The* (1939)
*Shining Hour, The* (1938)
*Mannequin* (1937)
*Last of Mrs. Cheyney, The* (1937)
*Bride Wore Red, The* (1937)
*Love on the Run* (1936)
*Gorgeous Hussy, The* (1936)
*No More Ladies* (1935)
*I Live My Life* (1935)
*Forsaking All Others* (1934)
*Chained* (1934)
*Sadie McKee* (1934)
*Dancing Lady* (1933)
*Today We Live* (1933)
*Rain* (1932)
*Letty Lynton* (1932)
*Grand Hotel* (1931)
*Possessed* (1931)
*This Modern Age* (1931)
*Laughing Sinners* (1931)
*Montana Moon* (1930)
*Paid* (1930)
*Our Blushing Brides* (1930)
*Dance, Fool, Dance* (1930)
*Hollywood Review of 1929* (1929)
*Untamed* (1929)
*Our Modern Maidens* (1929)
*The Duke Steps Out* (1929)
*Our Dancing Daughters* (1928)
*Dream of Love* (1928)
*Four Walls* (1928)
*Law of the Range, The* (1928)
*Across to Singapore* (1928)
*Rose Marie* (1928)
*West Point* (1928)
*Spring Fever* (1927)
*Twelve Miles Out* (1927)
*Unknown, The* (1927)
*Understanding Heart, The* (1927)
*Winners of the Wilderness* (1927)
*Taxi Dancer, The* (1927)
*Paris* (1926)
*Tramp, Tramp, Tramp* (1926)
*Boob, The* (1926)
*Sally, Irene and Mary* (1925)
*Old Clothes* (1925)
*Only Thing, The* (1925)
*Circle, The* (1925)
*Pretty Ladies* (1925)
*Lady of the Night* (1925)

### Bette Davis

*Wicked Stepmother* (1989)
*Whales of August, The* (1987)
*As Summers Die* (1986)
*Directed by William Wyler* (1986)
*Murder With Mirrors* (1985)
*Right of Way* (1983)

*Little Gloria...Happy at Last* (1982)
*Piano for Mrs. Cimino, A* (1982)
*Family Reunion* (1981)
*Skyward* (1980)
*Watcher in the Woods, The* (1980)
*White Mama* (1980)
*Strangers: The Story of a Mother and Daughter* (1979)
*Death on the Nile* (1978)
*Dark Secret of Harvest Home* (1978)
*Return from Witch Mountain* (1978)
*Burnt Offerings* (1976)
*Disappearance of Aimee, The* (1976)
*Scream, Pretty Peggy* (1973)
*Judge and Jake Wyler, The* (1972)
*Scopone Scientifico, Lo* (1972)
*Bunny O'Hare* (1971)
*Connecting Rooms* (1971)
*Madame Sin* (1971)
*Anniversary, The* (1968)
*Nanny, The* (1965)
*Hush...Hush, Sweet Charlotte* (1964)
*Where Love Has Gone* (1964)
*Noia, La* (1964)
*Dead Ringer* (1964)
*What Ever Happened to Baby Jane?* (1962)
*Pocketful of Miracles* (1961)
*Scapegoat, The* (1959)
*John Paul Jones* (1959)
*Catered Affair, The* (1956)
*Storm Center* (1956)
*Virgin Queen, The* (1955)
*Phone Call from a Stranger* (1952)
*Another Man's Poison* (1952)
*Star, The* (1952)
*Payment on Demand* (1951)
*All About Eve* (1950)
*Beyond the Forest* (1949)
*June Bride* (1948)
*Winter Meeting* (1948)
*Deception* (1946)
*Stolen Life, A* (1946)
*Corn Is Green, The* (1945)
*Hollywood Canteen* (1944)
*Mr. Skeffington* (1944)
*Old Acquaintance* (1943)
*Thank Your Lucky Stars* (1943)
*Watch on the Rhine* (1943)
*Show Business at War* (1943)
*Now, Voyager* (1942)
*In This Our Life* (1942)
*Little Foxes, The* (1941)
*Bride Came C.O.D., The* (1941)
*Great Lie, The* (1941)
*Man Who Came to Dinner, The* (1941)
*Shining Victory* (1941)
*Letter, The* (1940)
*All This, and Heaven Too* (1940)
*Private Lives of Elizabeth and Essex, The* (1939)
*Old Maid, The* (1939)
*Juarez* (1939)
*Dark Victory* (1939)
*Sisters, The* (1938)
*Jezebel* (1938)
*It's Love I'm After* (1937)
*That Certain Woman* (1937)
*Kid Galahad* (1937)
*Marked Woman* (1937)
*Satan Met a Lady* (1936)
*Golden Arrow, The* (1936)
*Petrified Forest, The* (1936)
*Dangerous* (1935)
*Special Agent* (1935)
*Front Page Woman* (1935)
*Girl from 10th Avenue, The* (1935)
*Bordertown* (1935)
*Housewife* (1934)
*Of Human Bondage* (1934)
*Fog Over Frisco* (1934)
*Jimmy the Gent* (1934)
*Big Shakedown, The* (1934)
*Fashions of 1934* (1934)
*Bureau of Missing Persons* (1933)
*Ex-Lady* (1933)
*Working Man, The* (1933)
*Parachute Jumper* (1933)
*20,000 Years in Sing Sing* (1933)
*Three on a Match* (1932)
*Cabin in the Cotton, The* (1932)
*Dark Horse, The* (1932)
*Rich Are Always with Us, The* (1932)
*So Big* (1932)
*Man Who Played God, The* (1932)
*Hell's House* (1932)
*Menace, The* (1932)
*Waterloo Bridge* (1931)
*Seed* (1931)
*Bad Sister* (1931)
*Way Back Home* (1931)

## Marlene Dietrich

*Entertaining the Troops* (1989)
*Going Hollywood: The War Years* (1988)
*Marlene* (1984)
*Just a Gigolo* (1979)
*Charlotte* (1974)
*Paris When It Sizzles*(1964)
*Black Fox, The* (1962)
*Judgment at Nuremberg* (1961)
*Touch of Evil* (1958)
*Witness for the Prosecution* (1957)
*Monte Carlo Story, The/Montecarlo* (1957)
*Around the World in Eighty Days* (1956)
*Rancho Notorious* (1952)
*No Highway in the Sky/ No Highway* (1951)
*Stage Fright* (1950)
*Jigsaw* (1949)
*Foreign Affair, A* (1948)
*Golden Earrings* (1947)
*Room Upstairs, The* (1946)
*Kismet* (1944)
*Follow the Boys* (1944)
*Spoilers, The* (1942)
*Pittsburgh* (1942)
*Lady Is Willing, The* (1942)
*Manpower* (1941)
*Flame of New Orleans, The* (1941)
*Seven Sinners* (1940)
*Destry Rides Again* (1939)
*Knight Without Armour* (1937)
*Angel* (1937)
*I Loved a Soldier* (1936)
*The Garden of Allah* (1936)
*Desire* (1936)
*Devil Is a Woman, The* (1935)
*Scarlet Empress, The (1934)*
*Song of Songs* (1933)
*Shanghai Express* (1932)
*Blonde Venus* (1932)
*Dishonored* (1931)
*Morocco* (1930)
*Blue Angel, The/Der Blaue Engel* (1930)
*The Ship of Lost Men/Das Schiff Der Verlorenen Menscher* (1929)
*Gefahren der Brautzeit* (1929)
*Die Frau Nach der Man Sich Sehnt* (1929)
*Prinzessin Olala* (1928)
*Ich Kusse Ihre Hand, Madame* (1928)
*Sein Grosster Bluff* (1927)
*Cafe Electric* (1927)
*Modern du Barry, A/Eine Dubarry von Heute* (1926)
*Manon Lescaut* (1926)
*Madame Wants No Children/ Madame Wonscht Keine Kinder* (1926)
*Kopf Hoch, Charly!* (1926)
*Der Juxbaron* (1926)
*The Joyless Street/Die Freudlöse Gasse/Street of Sorrow* (1925)
*Der Sprung Ins Leben* (1924)

*Tragodie der Liebe* (1923)
*Der Mensch Am Wege* (1923)
*Der Kleine Napoleon* (1923)

## Greta Garbo

*Two-Faced Woman* (1941)
*Ninotchka* (1939)
*Conquest* (1937)
*Camille* (1937)
*Anna Karenina* (1935)
*Painted Veil, The* (1934)
*Queen Christina* (1933)
*As You Desire Me* (1932)
*Grand Hotel* (1932)
*Mata Hari* (1931)
*Susan Lenox: Her Fall and Rise* (1931)
*Inspiration* (1931)
*Romance* (1930)
*Anna Christie* (1930)
*Kiss, The* (1929)
*Man's Man, A* (1929)
*Single Standard, The* (1929)
*Wild Orchids* (1929)
*Woman of Affairs, A* (1928)
*Mysterious Lady, The* (1928)
*Divine Woman, The* (1928)
*Love* (1927)
*Flesh and the Devil* (1927)
*Temptress, The* (1926)
*Torrent, The* (1926)
*Die Freudlöse Gasse (The Joyless Street)* (1925)
*Legend of Gosta Berling, The* (1924)
*Luffar-Petter (Peter the Tramp)* (1922)
*Our Daily Bread* (1922)
*How Not to Dress* (1921)

## Rita Hayworth

*Going Hollywood: The War Years* (1988)
*Circle* (1976)
*Wrath of God,The* (1972)
*Road to Salina* (1971)
*La Route de Salina* (1970)
*Naked Zoo, The* (1970)
*I Bastardi (1969)*
*Rover, The/El Avventuriero* (1967)
*L'avventuriero* (1967)
*Poppy Is Also a Flower, The* (1966)
*Money Trap, The* (1966)
*Love Goddesses, The* (1965)
*Circus World* (1964)
*Happy Thieves Producer, The* (1962)
*They Came to Cordura* (1959)
*Story on Page One, The* (1959)
*Separate Tables* (1958)
*Pal Joey* (1957)
*Fire Down Below* (1957)
*Miss Sadie Thompson* (1953)
*Salome* (1953)
*Affair in Trinidad* (1952)
*Lady from Shanghai, The* (1948)
*Loves of Carmen, The* (1948)
*Down to Earth* (1947)
*Gilda* (1946)
*Tonight and Every Night* (1945)
*Cover Girl* (1944)
*Tales of Manhattan* (1942)
*My Gal Sal* (1942)
*You Were Never Lovelier* (1942)
*Blood and Sand* (1941)
*Affectionately Yours* (1941)
*Strawberry Blonde, The* (1941)
*You'll Never Get Rich* (1941)
*Music in My Heart* (1940)
*Blondie on a Budget* (1940)
*Angels over Broadway* (1940)
*Susan and God* (1940)
*Lady in Question, The (1940)*
*Homicide Bureau* (1939)
*Renegade Ranger, The* (1939)
*Lone Wolf Spy Hunt, The* (1939)
*Only Angels Have Wings* (1939)
*There's Always a Woman* (1938)
*Who Killed Gail Preston?* (1938)
*Special Inspector* (1938)
*Juvenile Court* (1938)
*Convicted* (1938)
*Hit the Saddle* (1937)
*Shadow, The* (1937)
*Trouble in Texas* (1937)
*Old Louisiana* (1937)
*Criminals of the Air* (1937)
*The Game That Kills* (1937)
*Girls Can Play* (1937)
*Paid to Dance* (1937)
*Meet Nero Wolfe* (1936)
*Human Cargo* (1936)
*Rebellion* (1936)
*Caliente* (1935)
*Paddy O'Day* (1935)
*Under the Pampas Moon* (1935)
*Charlie Chan in Egypt* (1935)
*Dante's Inferno* (1935)
*Cruz Diablo* (1934)

## Marilyn Monroe

*Misfits, The* (1961)
*Let's Make Love* (1960)
*Some Like It Hot* (1959)
*Prince and the Showgirl, The* (1957)
*Bus Stop* (1956)
*Seven Year Itch, The* (1955)
*There's No Business Like Show Business* (1954)
*River of No Return* (1954)
*Niagara* (1953)
*How to Marry a Millionaire* (1953)
*Gentlemen Prefer Blondes* (1953)
*We're Not Married* (1952)
*Clash by Night* (1952)
*Don't Bother to Knock* (1952)
*Monkey Business* (1952)
*O. Henry's Full House* (1952)
*Love Nest* (1951)
*Let's Make It Legal* (1951)
*Hometown Story* (1951)
*As Young as You Feel* (1951)
*Ticket to Tomahawk, A* (1950)
*Right Cross* (1950)
*Fireball, The* (1950)
*Asphalt Jungle, The* (1950)
*All About Eve* (1950)
*Love Happy* (1949)
*Ladies of the Chorus* (1949)
*Scudda Hoo! Scudda Hay!* (1948)

## Pola Negri

*Moon-Spinners, The* (1964)
*Hi Diddle Diddle* (1943)
*Madame Bovary* (1937)
*Tango Notturno* (1937)
*Mazurka* (1935)
*Woman Commands, A* (1932)
*Barbed Wire* (1927)
*Hotel Imperial* (1927)
*Woman from Moscow, The* (1927)
*Crown of Lies, The* (1926)
*Good and Naughty* (1926)
*Flower of Night* (1925)
*Charmer, The* (1925)
*East of Suez* (1925)
*Woman of the World, A* (1925)
*Forbidden Paradise* (1924)
*Lily of the Dust* (1924)
*Cheat, The* (1923)
*Bella Donna* (1923)
*Montmartre* (1923)
*Hollywood* (1923)
*Spanish Dancer, The* (1923)
*Wildcat, The* (1921)
*Vendetta* (1921)
*Camille* (1920)

*One Arabian Night* (1920)
*Passion* (1919)
*Eyes of the Mummy, The* (1918)
*Gypsy Blood* (1918)

## Ingrid Pitt

*Helga Hanna's War* (1988)
*Transmutations* (1986)
*Wild Geese II* (1985)
*Final Option, The* (1982)
*Countess Dracula* (1972)
*House That Dripped Blood, The* (1970)
*Vampire Lovers* (1970)
*Where Eagles Dare* (1969)

## Barbara Steele

*Tief Oben* (1994)
*Silent Scream* (1980)
*Pretty Baby* (1978)
*Piranha* (1978)
*Le Cle sur la Porte* (1978)
*Space Watch Murders, The* (1978)
*Shivers* (1975)
*Caged Heat* (1974)
*Stop the World, I Want to Get Off* (1970)
*Honeymoon with a Stranger* (1969)
*Curse of the Crimson Altar, The* (1967)
*Young Torless* (1966)
*She-Beast, The* (1966)
*White Voices* (1965)
*Hours of Love, The* (1965)
*An Angel for Satan* (1965)
*Nightmare Castle* (1965)
*Terror Creatures from the Grave* (1965)
*Long Hair of Death, The* (1964)
*Les Baisers* (1964)
*Tre per una Rapina* (1964)
*Maniacs, The* (1964)
*Monocle, The* (1964)
*I Soldi* (1963)
*Castle of Blood* (1963)
*Il Capitano di Ferro* (1963)
*Sentimental Experiment* (1963)
*Ghost, The* (1963)
*8½* (1962)
*Terror of Dr. Hitchcock, The* (1962)
*Upstairs and Downstairs* (1961)
*Pit and the Pendulum, The* (1961)
*Black Sunday* (1960)
*Your Money or Your Wife* (1960)
*39 Steps, The* (1959)
*Sapphire* (1959)
*Bachelor of Hearts* (1958)

## Sharon Stone

*Last Dance* (1996)
*Diabolique* (1996)
*Casino* (1995)
*Specialist, The* (1994)
*Intersection* (1994)
*Quick and the Dead, The* (1994)
*Where Sleeping Dogs Lie* (1993)
*Hollywood Remembers: Harlow the Blonde Bombshell* (1993)
*Sliver* (1993)
*Diary of a Hitman* (1992)
*Basic Instinct* (1992)
*Scissors* (1991)
*He Said, She Said* (1991)
*Year of the Gun* (1991)
*Total Recall* (1990)
*Beyond the Stars* (1989)
*Blood and Sand* (1989)
*Above the Law* (1988)
*Tears in the Rain* (1988)
*Police Academy 4: Citizens on Patrol* (1987)
*Action Jackson* (1987)
*Cold Steel* (1987)
*Allan Quatermain and the Lost City of Gold* (1986)
*King Solomon's Mines* (1985)
*Irreconcilable Differences* (1984)

## Gloria Swanson

*Airport 1975* (1974)
*Chaplinesque, My Life and Hard Times* (1972)
*Mio Figlio Nerone* (also *Nero's Big Weekend*) (1956)
*Three for Bedroom C* (1952)
*Sunset Boulevard* (1950)
*Father Takes a Wife* (1941)
*Music in the Air* (1934)
*Perfect Understanding, A* (1933)
*Indiscreet* (1931)
*Tonight or Never* (1931)
*What a Widow!* (1930)
*Queen Kelly* (1929)
*Trespasser, The* (1929)
*Sadie Thompson* (1928)
*Love of Sunya,The* (1927)
*Untamed Lady, The (1926)*
*Fine Manners* (1926)
*Coast of Folly, The* (1925)
*Madame Sans-Gene* (1925)
*Stage Struck* (1925)
*Her Love Story* (1924)
*Manhandled* (1924)
*Humming Bird, The* (1924)
*Society Scandal, A* (1924)
*Wages of Virtue* (1924)
*Zaza* (1923)
*Bluebeard's Eighth Wife* (1923)
*Prodigal Daughters* (1923)
*Hollywood* (1923)
*Impossible Mrs. Bellew, The* (1922)
*Her Gilded Cage* (1922)
*Beyond the Rocks* (1922)
*Her Husband's Trademark* (1922)
*My American Wife* (1922)
*Don't Tell Everything* (1921)
*Great Moment, The* (1921)
*Affairs of Anatol, The* (1921)
*Under the Lash* (1921)
*Why Change Your Wife?* (1920)
*Something to Think About* (1920)
*For Better, For Worse* (1919)
*Don't Change Your Husband* (1919)
*Male and Female* (1919)
*Secret Code, The* (1918)
*Station Content* (1918)
*Shifting Sands* (1918)
*Everywoman's Husband* (1918)
*You Can't Believe Everything* (1918)
*Her Decision* (1918)
*Society for Sale* (1918)
*Wife or Country* (1918)
*Who's Baby?* (1917)
*Sultan's Wife, The* (1917)
*Dangers of a Bride* (1917)
*Baseball Madness* (1917)
*Teddy at the Throttle* (1917)
*Nick-of-Time Baby, The (1917)*
*Pullman Bride, A* (1917)
*Love on Skates* (1916)
*Danger Girl, The* (1916)
*Social Club, A* (1916)
*Hearts and Sparks* (1916)
*Dash of Courage, A* (1916)
*Haystacks and Steeples* (1916)
*Romance of an American Duchess, The* (1915)
*Sweedie Goes to College* (1915)
*Fable of Elvira and Farina and the Meal Ticket, The* (1915)
*His New Job* (1915)
*Ambition of the Baron, The* (1915)
*At the End of a Perfect Day* (1915)
*Broken Pledge, The* (1915)
*Song of the Soul, The* (1914)

# Videography

Some of the films listed below are truly wonderful—classics by any criterion. Others are camp classics, fun to watch, especially if you watch them with friends. Then there are those that leave more than a little be desired, but are notable because they have contributed in some way to the legendary image of the femme fatale.

Several of these films have been made and remade, featuring classic characters from history, literature, and mythology and starring some of the most famous actresses in cinema. Fanny Ward, Pola Negri, and Tallulah Bankhead have all starred in film versions of *The Cheat*, while actresses as diverse as Joan Crawford, Gloria Swanson, and Rita Hayworth have been featured in film adaptations of W. Somerset Maugham's *Rain*. Classic tales of vampire women have also been adapted for the screen, with images of Carmilla, the Countess Bathory, and Lilith recurring in film after film, with varying results.

The movies listed here scratch the surface of films dedicated to the fatal woman, but each will help to illustrate the many faces of the femme fatale—witch and siren, goddess and demon. To the best of my knowledge, all of these have been released on video. Since many are difficult to find, I've included a few alternative video sources, as well as some film and video guides to help you find even more interesting movies.

*The Addams Family*
1991. Barry Sonnenfeld. United States.
Based on the classic Charles Addams cartoons, this film stars Raul Julia and Anjelica Huston as Gomez and Morticia. Christina Ricci as daughter Wednesday is also delightful.

*Addams Family Values*
1993. Barry Sonnenfeld. United States.
Gomez and Morticia hire a serial-killing nanny to watch over new baby Pubert.

*The Addiction*
1995. Abel Ferrara. United States.
Lili Taylor plays a young college student horrified by the evil of the world and forced to confront her own evil when she is transformed into a vampire.

*All About Eve*
1950. Joseph Mankiewicz. United States.
This classic features Bette Davis as Margo Channing, the star who is about to be eclipsed by her scheming protégé. It also features Marilyn Monroe in an early role as a young starlet.

*And God Created Woman*
1957. Roger Vadim. France.
Vadim launched Brigitte Bardot's career in this film about a young nymphomaniac who is given a home by a local family with three young sons.

*Anna Christie*
1923. John Wray. United States.
Blanche Sweet plays a young girl who is sent away by her father, finds her way to Chicago, and becomes a prostitute. When she falls in love, she shares her story with her beau, hoping that he will understand.

*Anna Christie*
1930. Clarence Brown. United States.
Greta Garbo's first talking picture, the movie was advertised with the line "Garbo speaks!" Garbo plays a prostitute who falls in love with a sailor and does her best to keep her past a secret.

*The Atonement of Gosta Berling*
1924. Mauritz Stiller. Sweden.
A priest forced to leave the priesthood because of his drinking falls in love with a young married woman.

*The Awakening*
1980. Mike Newell. USA
This film is based on the novel *The Jewel of the Seven Stars* a by Bram Stoker. An archeologist finds the tomb of an evil Egyptian princess, setting lose her soul, which then tries to claim the body of the archeologist's daughter.

*Barbarella*
1968. Roger Vadim. France.
Based on a popular French sci-fi comic strip, *Barbarella* features Jane Fonda as the space-traveling nymphette and Anita Pallenberg as the evil queen. This film helped to inspire Forrest J. Ackerman and Jim Warren in their creation of the vampire with a heart of gold, Vampirella.

*Basic Instinct*
1992. Paul Verhoeven. United States.
Sharon Stone stars as Catherine Trammel, who is suspected of being an icepick-wielding murderess and who seduces Nick Curran (Michael Douglas), the detective assigned to the case. Although conceived as a star vehicle for Michael Douglas, Stone's performance—as well as the infamous interrogation scene—launched her to international stardom.

*Batman Returns*
1992. Tim Burton. United States.
Michelle Pfeiffer stars as Selina Kyle, a.k.a. Catwoman, complete with latex catsuit. The television role was played by Eartha Kitt in the last season.

*Bell, Book and Candle*
1958. Richard Quine. United States.
Kim Novak stars as the witch who has decided not to use her powers but changes her mind when an interesting and attractive young man (James Stewart) moves into the building.

*Belle de Jour*
1967. Luis Bu1uel. France.
Catherine Deneuve is the repressed newlywed who finds sexual fulfillment by becoming a daytime prostitute.

*Betty Blue*
1986. Jean-Jacques Beineix. France.
A young woman's manic-depression pushes her lover into a downward spiral of poverty, violence, and insanity.

*Black Sunday*
1960. Mario Bava. Italy.
Barbara Steele stars as both Princess Ada and as Princess Katia in this tale of a vampiric witch who has sworn vengeance on her executioners and tries to take over the body of her granddaughter to achieve her goals.

*Black Widow*
1987. Bob Rafelson. United States.
A federal agent is on the trail of a murderer who marries rich men and then kills them.

*Blonde Venus*
1932. Josef von Sternberg. United States.
Marlene Dietrich plays a former cabaret singer whose a marriage is threatened when she gets a job as a nightclub performer to pay the bills.

*Blood and Roses* (or *Et Mourir de Plaisir*)
1961. Roger Vadim. France.
Annette Vadim is Carmilla in this updated version of Le Fanu's vampire tale.

*Blood and Sand*
1922. Fred Niblo. United States.
Nita Naldi and Rudolph Valentino star in this silent Spanish romance about a matador torn between two women, one his childhood sweetheart, the other a hot-blooded siren.

*Blood and Sand*
1941. Rouben Mamoulian. United States.
Rita Hayworth and Tyrone Power star in this remake of the 1922 film. Hayworth made the transition from the leading man's romantic interest to sultry star with her performance.

*Blood and Sand*
1989. Javier Elorrieta. United States.
Sharon Stone's reprise of the role made famous by Rita Hayworth.

*Blood of Dracula*
1957. Herbert L. Strock. England.
An unpopular female student is turned into a vampire by an attentive female chemistry teacher. Part of the "I Was a Teenage . . ." series.

*Blood-Spattered Bride* (also *Blood Castle, La Novia Ensangrentada*)
1972. Vincente Aranda. Spain.
A newlywed couple returns to the husband's family estate, where the bride discovers a portrait of a faceless woman in a bloodied wedding gown. The woman portrayed in the painting returns in the flesh, encouraging the bride to kill her abusive husband.

*The Blue Angel*
1930. Josef von Sternberg. Germany.
A repressed professor goes to a local nightclub and falls in love with Lola Lola, played by Marlene Dietrich. Amused by the awkward professor, she marries him and bit by bit strips him of his dignity and self-respect.

*Blue Velvet*
1986. David Lynch. United States.
This disturbing film explores sterile suburbia and its seamy underside. Laura Dern and Isabella Rossellini are a study in light and dark, with Dern as the innocent suburbanite and Rossellini as the abused mistress of an underworld kingpin.

*Body Heat*
1981. Lawrence Kasdan. United States.
Kathleen Turner seduces a young lawyer and involves him in a plot to kill her husband.

*Bordello of Blood* (also *Tales from the Crypt Presents Bordello of Blood*)
1996. Gilbert Adler. United States.
This is a sophomoric comedy about a detective on the trail of a missing teenager who finds himself in a gothic-style brothel presided over by the vampire queen Lilith (Angie Everhart) and a bevy of vampire babes.

*Born to Be Bad*
1950. Nicholas Ray. United States.
Joan Fontaine plays an opportunistic woman who attempts to steal another woman's husband while carrying on a love affair of her own.

*Bound*
1996. Larry and Andy Wachowski. United States.
A gangster's wife and a female ex-con conspire to steal two million dollars of the mob's money that is in her husband's keeping.

*Bram Stoker's Dracula*
1992. Francis Ford Coppola. United States.
The gorgon-like "brides" of Dracula, the sexually aggressive Lucy and the newly awakened Mina, are interesting variations on the traditional characters in this visually striking film.

*The Bride Wore Black*
1968. François Truffaut. France.
Jeanne Moreau stars as a young woman whose husband is accidentally killed on their wedding day. The bride exacts her revenge by tracking down the five men involved in his death and killing them one by one.

*The Bride Wore Red*
1937. Dorothy Arzner. United States.
Joan Crawford stars as a cabaret singer who pretends to be a wealthy socialite in order to seduce a wealthy aristocrat.

*The Brides of Dracula*
1960. Terence Fisher. England.
An innocent French governess frees a vampire, which results in a rash of vampire attacks at a nearby girls' school.

*Buffy, the Vampire Slayer*
1992. Fran Rubel Kazui. United States.
A high-school cheerleader discovers that she is next in a long line of vampire hunters. This film inspired a television series that has been heralded for providing one of the few positive media role models for girls.

*Bulletproof Heart*
1995. Mark Malone. United States.
A hitman falls in love with the beautiful socialite he's been ordered to kill.

*Burn, Witch, Burn*
1962. Sidney Hayers. United States.
A college professor is horrified to find out that he owes his success to his wife's witchcraft. When he convinces her to renounce her dark ways, other campus witches appear to take advantage of the opportunity. Based on Fritz's Leiber novella *Conjure Wife*.

*Camille*
1921. Fred Niblo. United States.
Alla Nazimova stars as the dying courtesan who falls in love with a shallow young nobleman.

*Camille*
1936. George Cukor. United States.
Greta Garbo is the dying courtesan in this remake, which is now considered one of her finest films.

*Carmen*
1983. Carlos Saura. Spain.
The story of Carmen is updated in the flamenco version of the superstitious gypsy and her doomed love affair with Don José.

*Carmilla*
1990. Gabriella Beaumont. United States.
This made-for-cable movie, starring Ione Skye and Meg Tilly, is based on the novella *Carmilla*, but it also draws elements from *Christabel*. The story is moved from the dark castle in Styria to a post-Civil War southern plantation.

*Castle of Blood* (also *Castle of Terror*)
1964. Anthony Dawson. Italy.
A poet is forced to stay the night in a haunted castle. Barbara Steele appears as Lady Blackwood, one of the ghosts that dwell within the castle's walls.

*Cat Girl*
1957. Alfred Shaughnessy. England.
Hammer Studios horror queen Barbara Shelley stars as a woman who has inherited the family curse—a psychic link with a ferocious leopard.

*Cat People*
1942. Jacques Tourneur. England.
A young newlywed woman, played by Simone Simon, fears that she will turn into a ferocious panther when sexually aroused.

*Cat People*
1982. Paul Schrader. United States.
A young woman discovers that she turns into a ferocious panther when sexually aroused and that she can only safely mate with her estranged brother.

*The Cheat*
1915. Cecil B. DeMille. United States.
Fannie Ward stars in the first of three versions of this film concerning a society wife who gambles and then loses a thousand dollars and must suffer the consequences.

*A Chinese Ghost Story*
1987. Ching Siu Tung. Hong Kong.
A young tax collector falls in love with a beautiful woman, only to discover that she is a ghost eternally bound to a vampiric tree spirit.

*Cinderella*
1950. Wilfred Jackson, Hamilton Luske, Clyde Geronimi. United States.
Cinderella's wicked stepmother and her two wicked stepsisters are the witchly trio in this Disney fairy tale.

*Cleopatra*
1934. Cecil B. DeMille. United States.
Claudette Colbert is featured as Cleopatra.

*Cleopatra*
1963. Joseph Mankiewicz. United States.
Elizabeth Taylor and Richard Burton star as Cleopatra and Anthony.

*Cobra Woman*
1944. Robert Siodmak. United States.
A queen of a cobra-worshiping jungle tribe is challenged by her evil twin sister. Maria Montez plays both sisters.

*Coquette*
1929. Sam Taylor. United States.
This was Mary Pickford's first talking picture. Pickford is a flirtatious flapper whose father kills her boyfriend and then commits suicide.

*Countess Dracula*
1971. Peter Sasdy. England.
This horror thriller stars Ingrid Pitt as the Countess Bathory, who accidentally discovers that bathing in the blood of virgins will keep her young.

*The Craft*
1996. Andrew Fleming. United States.
A troubled teenager in a new school befriends three outcasts who like to dabble in witchcraft.

*Cult of the Cobra*
1955. Francis D. Lyon. England.
Servicemen witness the secret rites of an ancient cobra cult and are then stalked by the snake goddess in human form.

*Curse of the Cat People*
1944. Robert Wise, Gunther von Fristch. United States.
A young girl is aided by the spirit of her dead mother in this sequel to *Cat People*.

*Curse of the Crying Woman* (also *MaldiciMn de la Llorona*)
1961. Rafael BaledRn. Mexico.
A vampire woman and her husband attempt to revive the spirit of La Llorona, the weeping woman of Mexican folklore.

*Dancing Lady*
1933. Robert Z. Leonard. United States.
Joan Crawford plays a young dancer striving for stardom.

*Dangerous*
1935. Alfred E. Green. United States.
Bette Davis won an Oscar for her portrayal of an alcoholic actress redeemed by the love of a good man.

*Dangerous Liaisons* (or *Les Liaisons Dangereuses*)
1960. Roger Vadim. France.
Jeanne Moreau and Annette Vadim star in this updated version of the eighteenth-century novel.

*Dangerous Liaisons*
1988. Stephen Frears. United States.
Glenn Close, Michelle Pfeiffer, and John Malkovich star in this costume drama in which two decadent aristocrats (Close and Malkovich) spend their time manipulating and deceiving others. Michelle Pfeiffer is the innocent newlywed caught in the game.

*The Dark Angel*
1991. Peter Hammond. England.
Beatie Edney is the innocent heiress who lives with her eccentric and eerie Uncle Silas. Jane Lapotaire is the haunting and drug-addicted governess.

*Dark Shadows*
1966–67. John Sedwick and Lela Swift. United States.
The TV soap opera about the vampire Barnabas Collins who chooses a local girl to be his wife.

*Daughters of Darkness* (or *La Rouge aux Levres*)
1971. Harry Kumel. Belgium.
A couple on their honeymoon stop at a Belgian hotel, where they meet the Countess Bathory and her female companion, Ilona.

*Deception*
1946. Irving Rapper. United States.
Bette Davis stars as a pianist torn between two loves, her sponsor and her cellist boyfriend.

*Deceptions*
1990. Reuben Preuss. United States.
An erotic thriller about a wealthy woman who kills her husband and the detective assigned to investigate the case.

*Def by Temptation*
1990. James Bond III. United States.
A young man in ministerial school is seduced by a succubus.

*Desire*
1936. Frank Borzage. United States.
Marlene Dietrich is a jewel thief who involves an innocent tourist (Gary Cooper) in smuggling her loot across national borders. In the midst of the adventures, the two fall in love.

*Desperado*
1995. Robert Rodriguez. United States.
Salma Hayek is a bookstore owner who joins Antonio

Banderas (El Mariachi) in his pursuit of an infamous drug lord.

*Desperately Seeking Susan*
1985. Susan Seidelman. United States.
Rosanna Arquette stars as a bored housewife who finds excitement in the personal ads, becoming obsessed with a series of ads between a man and a woman named Susan (Madonna). When she is injured, she loses her memory, and, believing she is Susan, begins living the life she's been fantasizing about.

*Diabolique*
1955. Henri-Georges Cluzot. France.
The mistress and the wife of an abusive schoolmaster plot to kill him, then carry out their plan and wait while the investigation into his disappearance takes place.

*Diabolique*
1996. Jeremiah S. Chechik. United States.
This remake of the 1955 classic stars Sharon Stone as the mistress.

*Diary of a Lost Girl*
1929. G. W. Pabst. Germany.
Louise Brooks stars in her second film directed by Pabst in which a young German woman lives a life of degradation and despair.

*Disclosure*
1994. Barry Levinson. United States.
Michael Douglas plays a family man who is sexually harassed by his new boss, who is also a former lover.

*The Divorce of Lady X*
1938. Tim Whelan. England.
A spoiled debutante (Merle Oberon) assumes a false identity in order to seduce a misogynistic divorce lawyer.

*The Divorcee*
1930. Robert Z. Leonard. United States.
Norma Shearer is out to beat her husband at philandering.

*Dr. Jekyll and Sister Hyde*
1971. Roy Ward Baker. England.
In this variation on a theme, Dr. Jekyll's doppelganger is a murderous woman who murders prostitutes to excise their ovaries and use the estrogen for experiments.

*Dolores Claiborne*
1994. Taylor Hackford. United States.
A young woman (Jennifer Jason Leigh) returns to her hometown when her mother (Kathy Bates) is accused of murdering an old woman for whom she had been caring.

*Double Indemnity*
1944. Billy Wilder. United States.
An insurance agent is seduced by a woman (Barbara Stanwyck) who wants him to kill her husband. A classic noir drama.

*Dracula*
1931. Tod Browning. United States.
This is the first screen adaptation of Bram Stoker's novel approved by Florence Stoker.

*Dracula's Daughter*
1936. Lambert Hillyer. United States.
The Countess Marya Zaleska (Gloria Holden), Dracula's daughter, is the unwilling inheritor of her father's curse.

*Dracula's Widow*
1988. Christopher Coppola. United States.
Sylvia Kristel is the lonely widow in search of a new companion.

*Dubarry*
1930. Sam Taylor. United States.
Norma Talmadge is Madame Dubarry, the French mistress of Louis XV.

*Duel in the Sun*
1946. King Vidor. United States.
A Western with Jennifer Jones as a mixed-race woman and Gregory Peck and Joseph Cotten as the two brothers who come to blows in their competition for her attentions.

*The Dybbuk*
1937. Michael Waszynski. United States.
A Yiddish film in which a newlywed woman is possessed by a restless spirit.

*Ed Wood*
1994. Tim Burton. United States.
The story of Ed Wood and his filmmaking career stars model and actress Lisa Marie as Vampira.

*Elvira, Mistress of the Dark*
1988. James Signorelli. United States.
A camp classic with Elvira as the child of a sorceress who inherits a house in a conservative Massachusetts town and the chaos that ensues when she moves in.

*Embrace of the Vampire*
1995. Anne Goursaud. United States.
Goursaud, who directed many episodes of the *Red Shoe Diaries*, directs Alyssa Milano in this tale of a virginal young woman who is torn between her morals and her budding sensuality when she is pursued by her well-

intentioned boyfriend and the vampire who believes her to be the incarnation of his long-lost love.

*Excalibur*
1981. John Boorman. England.
An epic retelling of the legends of King Arthur with Helen Mirren as the seductive and entrancing Morgana le Fey.

*Fascination*
1985. Jean Rollin. France.
A coven of women comes together to drink the blood of a shared victim.

*Fatal Attraction*
1987. Adrian Lyne. United States.
Michael Douglas and Glenn Close embark on a short-lived and torrid affair, resulting in a downward spiral of violence and abuse.

*Flesh and the Devil*
1927. Clarence Brown. United States.
Greta Garbo is the married woman whose seductive allure causes a duel between two friends, one of them her husband, who is killed. Banished, her lover asks his best friend to look after her, and he, too, falls in love with her.

*A Fool There Was*
1915. Frank Powell. United States.
Theda Bara as the vampire who seduces diplomat John Schuyler, leading him to abandon his wife, his child, and his government position, and, finally, to his ruin.

*Freaks*
1932. Tod Browning. United States.
A cult classic about a troupe of circus freaks who exact revenge on a beautiful aerialist who marries a midget for his money and her lover, the strongman. Silent film vamp Olga Baclanova stars as the aerialist who meets her own freakish demise as a result of her scheming ways.

*Fright Night*
1985. Tom Holland. United States.
A teenager suspects that his new neighbor is a vampire and enlists the aid of a local television horror host to battle the monster. His girlfriend, played by Amanda Bearse, is seduced by the vampire and becomes a vampire herself.

*Fright Night II*
1988. Tommy Lee Wallace. United States.
Julie Carmen stars as the vampire out to avenge her brother's death in this sequel to *Fright Night*.

*The Frighteners*
1996. Peter Jackson. United States.
This horror comedy stars Dee Wallace Stone as (finally!) the femme fatale.

*Le Frisson des Vampires*
1970. Jean Rollin. France.
A honeymooning couple find themselves moored in a medieval castle inhabited by two aging hippies and their vampire mistress, a "butch" bisexual vampire in leather and chains.

*From Dusk Till Dawn*
1995. Richard Rodriguez. United States.
Reptilian vampires in a biker bar in Mexico wreak havoc on those not wise enough to leave the bar before dusk. Salma Hayek is the vampire queen whose stage show includes an erotic dance with a snake.

*Gentlemen Prefer Blondes*
1953. Howard Hawks. United States.
Marilyn Monroe stars as the sweet but gold-digging Lorelei Lee. Jane Russell plays her sidekick.

*Gilda*
1946. Charles Vidor. United States.
Rita Hayworth stars in this highly charged love triangle among casino owner Macready, his assistant Johnny, and the casino owner's wife, Gilda.

*The Girl with the Hungry Eyes*
1994. Jon Jacobs. United States.
A model commits suicide in a fashionable hotel in 1937, returning as a vampire to haunt (and taunt) the resident of the now-derelict building.

*The Gorgon*
1964. Terence Fisher. England.
The gorgon survives in pre-World War II Germany, living as a lovely doctor's assistant by day and turning men to stone by night.

*Gothic*
1987. Ken Russell. England.
Ken Russell's surreal imagery provides the backdrop for this version of the night Percy Shelley, Mary Shelley, Lord Byron, and John Polidori began telling a series of ghost stories.

*Greed*
1924. Erich von Stroheim. United States.
A woman's obsession with money drives her husband to murder. ZaSu Pitts plays the mad wife who, having hoarded large amounts of money, pours it out on the bed and rolls about in the bills and coins.

*The Grifters*
1990. Stephen Frears. United States.
Anjelica Huston, Annette Bening, and John Cusack star in this tale of the intricate web of deceit that binds the three con artists.

*Gypsy Blood*
1918. Ernst Lubitsch. Germany.
Pola Negri is Carmen in one of many silent film versions of Bizet's opera.

*The Hand That Rocks the Cradle*
1992. Curtis Hanson. United States.
Rebecca DeMornay is the nanny who plots to take over the lives of the family for whom she works.

*Haunted*
1995. Lewis Gilbert. England.
A parapsychologist (Aidan Quinn) is invited to a English mansion to investigate supernatural occurrences. While there, he has visions of his twin sister, who died as a child, and is seduced by the mysterious woman who lives in the mansion with her brother and their elderly nanny.

*How to Marry a Millionaire*
1953. Jean Negulesco. United States.
Marilyn Monroe, Betty Grable, and Lauren Bacall star in this comedy about three women who hatch a plan to marry millionaires.

*The Hunchback of Notre Dame*
1923. Wallace Worsley. United States.
Patsy Ruth Miller is Esmeralda and Lon Chaney, Sr. is Quasimodo in the silent screen version of Victor Hugo's novel about the bellringer who lives in the cathedral and the condemned gypsy woman he loves.

*The Hunchback of Notre Dame*
1939. William Dieterle. United States.
Maureen O'Hara is Esmeralda and Charles Laughton is Quasimodo.

*The Hunchback of Notre Dame*
1957. Jean Delannoy. United States.
Gina Lollobrigida is Esmeralda and Anthony Quinn is Quasimodo.

*The Hunchback of Notre Dame*
1982. Michael Tuchner. United States.
Leslie Anne Downs is Esmeralda and Anthony Hopkins is Quasimodo in this made-for-television classic tale.

*The Hunchback of Notre Dame*
1996. Kirk Wise, Gary Trousdale. United States.
Disney's animated version of this French drama has Demi Moore as the voice of Esmeralda and Timothy Hutton doing the voice of Quasimodo. Although given a happy ending for the benefit of the children in the audience, the story is still imbued with passion, lust, and violence.

*The Hunger*
1983. Tony Scott. United States.
An ancient vampire (Catherine Deneuve), aware that her lover and companion (David Bowie) is dying, pursues the female doctor (Susan Sarandon) he has enlisted to help stop his aging process.

*Hush . . . Hush, Sweet Charlotte*
1965. Robert Aldrich. United States.
This film was originally intended as another Joan Crawford/Bette Davis vehicle following the success of *What Ever Happened to Baby Jane?* An aging southern belle finds out the truth about her fiancé's murder when the case is re-opened thirty-seven years after his death. Crawford's role was eventually played by Olivia de Havilland.

*I Married a Witch*
1942. René Clair. United States.
A romantic comedy in which a woman (Veronica Lake) burned at the stake during the Salem witch trials returns to haunt the descendants of one of her accusers, but ends up falling in love.

*I Walked with a Zombie*
1943. Jacques Tourneur. United States.
A young American nurse goes to Haiti to care for the catatonic wife of a plantation owner who lives with his alcoholic brother and their domineering mother. She falls in love with the husband, and in an effort to bring him happiness, takes his wife to a voodoo ceremony to be healed.

*Innocent Blood*
1992. John Landis. United States.
Vampire Marie (Anne Parillaud) gets mixed up with the Mafia when she accidentally turns a mob boss into a vampire.

*Interview with the Vampire*
1994. Neil Jordan. United States.
This is the much-talked-about film version of Anne Rice's first novel. Kirsten Dunst is Claudia, the adult vampire trapped in a child's body who lures her victims with a mixture of ostensible youthful innocence and seduction.

*Irma Vep*
1997. Olivier Assayas. France.
Maggie Cheung plays herself in this story of making a film based on the silent-film serial in which a seductive cat

burglar known as Irma Vep (an anagram of "vampire") leads a gang of jewel thieves know as *Les Vampires*.

*Island of Dr. Moreau*
1977. William Whitney. United States.
A researcher is stranded on a remote island where scientist Moreau is conducting genetic experiments with animals and turning them into the humanlike creatures that inhabit the island. Barbara Carrera is the Panther Woman.

*Island of Dr. Moreau*
1996. John Frankenheimer. United States.
This all-star remake of the 1932 classic stars Marlon Brando as Dr. Moreau and Val Kilmer as his assistant. Faruza Balk is the Panther Woman.

*Island of Lost Souls*
1932. Erle C. Kenton. United States.
Still considered a classic, *Island of Lost Souls* features Charles Laughton as the maniacal Dr. Moreau and Kathleen Burke as Lota, the Panther Woman. Burke beat out more than 60,000 women in the national search for the woman who would play Lota because of her "naturally feline" features.

*It*
1927. Clarence Badger. United States.
Clara Bow plays the "It" girl in this movie based on the Elinor Glyn novel of the same name.

*Jade*
1995. William Friedkin. United States.
Screenwriter Joe Esterhasz (*Basic Instinct*) returns to familiar territory in this story of a devious wife suspected of killing her rich lover.

*Jezebel*
1938. William Wyler. United States.
Bette Davis, who won an Oscar for her performance, plays a tempestuous southern belle who loses her fiancé when she tries to make him jealous.

*Johnny Guitar*
1953. Nicholas Ray. United States.
This camp classic stars saloon owner Joan Crawford and reformist Mercedes McCambridge going head-to-head in a battle over the guitar player they both love.

*Lair of the White Worm*
1988. Ken Russell. England.
Russell's typical surreal style is perfect for the over-the-top interpretation of Bram Stoker's over-the-top novel concerning a cold, calculating woman who worships a wormlike creature, luring innocent bystanders as human sacrifices to the ancient Celtic deity.

*The Last Seduction*
1994. John Dahl. United States.
Linda Fiorentino stars as the ruthless Bridget, who talks her husband into a crooked pharmaceutical drug deal and then runs off with the money.

*Lemora, Lady Dracula*
1973. Richard Blackburn. United States.
A young choir girl is drawn into the lair of Lady Dracula.

*The Leopard Woman*
1920. Wesley H. Ruggles. United States
Silent-screen vamp Louise Glaum is the leopard woman in this tropical thriller.

*Lifeboat*
1944. Alfred Hitchcock. United States.
Tallulah Bankhead shines as the self-absorbed socialite stranded in a lifeboat with seven other mismatched survivors of a German U-boat attack on an oceanliner.

*Lifeforce*
1985. Tobe Hooper. United States.
Colin Wilson's *The Space Vampires* is adapted for film in this tale of an alien creature who, in the form of beautiful woman, sucks the life energy out of her victims, leaving only dry husks of the victims' former selves.

*The Little Foxes*
1941. William Wyler. United States.
Bette Davis stars in the role of Regina (made famous on stage by Tallulah Bankhead), the vicious southern belle who destroys everyone around her in her pursuit of power.

*Little Minister*
1934. Richard Wallace. United States.
Katharine Hepburn is the gypsy girl who wins the heart of a parish minister who thinks she is the local earl's daughter.

*Lolita*
1962. Stanley Kubrick. United States.
A middle-aged professor is obsessed with a young girl (a "nymphette"), leading to the destruction of them both. Based on the novel by Vladimir Nabokov.

*The Love Goddesses*
1965. Saul J. Turell. United States.
A television documentary examining the lives and careers of the "love goddesses" of the silver screen.

*The Loves of Carmen*
1948. Charles Vidor. United States.
Rita Hayworth stars in this film version of Bizet's opera *Carmen*.

*Lust for a Vampire* (or *To Love a Vampire*)
1970. Jimmy Sangster. England.
The second in the Hammer Studios Carmilla trilogy. Carmilla haunts a girls finishing school, abducting both teachers and students.

*Madame Sin*
1971. David Greene. United States.
Bette Davis stars in her first made-for-television movie about a plot to use a nuclear submarine to take over the world.

*Mamma Dracula*
1988. Boris Szulzinger. France.
The Countess Bathory needs a blood substitute to continue her undead existence but is interrupted by the arrival of the vampire hunter, Nancy Hawaii.

*Mark of the Vampire*
1935. Tod Browning. United States.
This remake of *London After Midnight* stars Bela Lugosi and Carroll Borland as Count Mora and his daughter. A mysterious wound on Count Mora's right temple is all that is left of an original subplot that involved the incestuous relationship between the count and his daughter. The count murders his daughter and then commits suicide, and both father and daughter return from the grave as vampires.

*Mata Hari*
1932. George Fitzmaurice. United States.
Greta Garbo stars as a German spy who steals secrets from the French by using her beauty and sensuality as a lure.

*Metropolis*
1926. Fritz Lang. Germany.
A dark fantasy about a future technology-obsessed society governed by the heartless robotrix Ultima Futura played by Brigitte Helm.

*Mildred Pierce*
1945. Michael Curtiz. United States.
Joan Crawford plays a divorced mother competing with her daughter for a man's love.

*Miss Sadie Thompson*
1953. Curtis Bernhardt. United States.
This 3-D musical version of the W. Somerset Maugham story stars Rita Hayworth. Previous versions include *Rain* (with Joan Crawford) and *Sadie Thompson* (with Gloria Swanson).

*Mr. Skeffington*
1944. Vincent Sherman. United States.
Bette Davis is a spoiled socialite who marries for convenience, abuses her husband, and still manages to get rich from a hefty divorce settlement.

*Morocco*
1930. Josef von Sternberg. United States.
Marlene Dietrich makes her American film debut as a world-weary nightclub singer in love with a French foreign legion officer.

*Nadja*
1994. Michael Almereyda. United States.
Nadja is the daughter of Count Dracula who wanders the streets of Manhattan in search of her brother.

*The Nanny*
1965. Seth Holt. England.
A nanny (Bette Davis) and her young charge engage in a battle of wills.

*Near Dark*
1987. Kathryn Bigelow. United States.
A graphic vampire Western in which a young man falls in love with a slight and somber young woman who is traveling with a band of vampires, one of whom is a veteran of the Civil War.

*Niagara*
1952. Henry Hathaway. United States.
A scheming wife (Marilyn Monroe) plans to kill her husband (Joseph Cotten) in the legendary honeymoon tourist spot.

*Of Human Bondage*
1934. John Cromwell. United States.
From the W. Somerset Maugham novel about a doctor who falls in love with a volatile and abusive waitress, played by Bette Davis.

*Once Bitten*
1985. Howard Storm. United States.
Lauren Hutton is the vampire in this teen horror comedy.

*101 Dalmations*
1961. Clyde Geronimi, Wolfgang Reitherman, Hamilton Luske. United States.
Dog owners Roger and Anita are dismayed when their puppies are kidnapped by the villainous Cruella De Vil, who wants to make a fabulous spotted fur coat.

*101 Dalmations*
1996. Stephen Herek. United States.
This live-action remake of the 1961 animated children's

movie stars Glenn Close as Cruella De Vil. Cruella's great costumes and hair make the film worth viewing.

*Orgy of the Vampires* (also *Vampire's Night Orgy*)
1973. Leon Klimovsky. United States.
An Ed Wood production including footage of Vampira originally filmed for *Plan 9 from Outer Space.*

*Pandora's Box*
1928. G. W. Pabst. Germany.
Louise Brooks plays the siren whose presence leads those around her to self-destruction.

*Plan 9 from Outer Space*
1956. Ed Wood. United States.
Vampira makes a cameo appearance in this film about aliens who reanimate the dead in order to take over the earth.

*The Postman Always Rings Twice*
1946. Tay Garnett. United States.
Lana Turner stars as the bored wife of a gas station owner who falls in love with a drifter. The two of them then hatch to kill her husband.

*The Postman Always Rings Twice*
1981. Bob Rafelson. United States.
This remake of the 1946 classic stars Jessica Lange and Jack Nicholson. Although more graphic than the original, it lacks much of its style.

*Praying Mantis*
1993. James Keach. United States.
Jane Seymour, in the tradition of the insect that eats her mates, marries and then kills her husbands. Frances Fisher is the sister of fiancé number six, and she doesn't have a good feeling about her new sister-in-law to be.

*Princess Tam Tam*
1935. Edmond T. Greville. France.
A French *My Fair Lady* in which a beautiful African woman (Josephine Baker) is Europeanized and introduced by her mentor to "polite" society as a princess.

*Prizzi's Honor*
1985. John Huston. United States.
Jack Nicholson plays a hitman who falls in love with a woman (Kathleen Turner) who turns out to be a hired gun for a competing mob family.

*Queen Bee*
1955. Ronald MacDougall. United States.
Joan Crawford is a spiteful southern belle who tries to interfere with her husband's new romance, even as she pursues an outside romance of her own.

*Queen Christina*
1933. Rouben Mamoulian. United States.
Greta Garbo stars as the legendary Queen Christina, a seventeenth-century bisexual woman who relinquishes the throne for love.

*Queen Kelly*
1928. Erich von Stroheim. United States.
A convent girl (Gloria Swanson) is seduced by a prince and later sent to her aunt's brothel in Africa. Footage from *Queen Kelly* was later used in Sunset Boulevard.

*The Quick and the Dead*
1995. Sam Raimi. United States.
This stylish Western stars Sharon Stone as a lone gunslinger out to avenge her father's death.

*Rain*
1932. Lewis Milestone. United States.
Joan Crawford is a prostitute servicing marines on a South Pacific island, where she meets a minister who falls in love with her and wants her to "redeem" herself.

*Rebecca*
1940. Alfred Hitchcock. United States.
A young woman marries a mysterious older gentleman, and, returning to his family estate, finds the spirit of his first wife still present. Dame Judith Anderson plays Mrs. Danvers, the ominous and omnipresent housekeeper determined to keep the memory of Rebecca alive.

*Red-Headed Woman*
1932. Jack Conway. United States.
Jean Harlow stars as a conniving woman who comes between her boss and his wife and, after marrying her boss, continues her wanton seduction of the men in her life.

*Red Rock West*
1993. John Dahl. United States.
Nicholas Cage stars as an out-of-luck and out-of-money drifter who is mistaken for a hitman and seduced by the woman he is supposed to kill (Lara Flynn Boyle).

*Romeo Is Bleeding*
1993. Peter Medak. United States.
Gary Oldman is a police detective who identifies a federally protected witness for a local mob boss. Lena Olin is the hitwoman who proves too much a match for the crooked cop.

*Sadie Thompson*
1928. Raoul Walsh. United States.
Gloria Swanson is the prostitute in the South Seas in this silent-film version of W. Somerset Maugham's *Rain.*

*Samson and Delilah*
1950. Cecile B. DeMille. United States.
After being rejected by Samson, the infuriated Delilah learns the secret of Samson's strength and plans his ultimate demise.

*Scarlet Street*
1945. Fritz Lang. United States.
A mild-mannered man (Edward G. Robinson) is driven to embezzle to please the manipulative woman (Joan Bennett) with whom he has fallen in love.

*Season of the Witch* (or *Hungry Wives*)
1973. George A. Romero. United States.
A frustrated housewife becomes intrigued with witchcraft, and as she develops her skills, finds herself increasingly estranged from her controlling husband.

*Seduced by Evil*
1994. Tony Wharmby. United States.
Suzanne Somers is surprisingly interesting in this story of a journalist on the trail of a shaman who recognizes her as the reincarnation of a Brazilian woman who was his lover in a former life.

*The Sentinal*
1976. Michael Winner. United States.
A model moves into an old brownstone, meets her deranged neighbors, and discovers that she has been chosen to be the next guardian of the gates of Hell.

*Serpent's Lair*
1995. Jeff Reiner. United States.
Tom and Alex have just moved into their dream apartment, but it has a haunted past, and Tom is drawn into the web of the local femme fatale who goes by the name of Lilith.

*She*
1925. Leander de Cordova. England.
Betty Blythe is the immortal Queen Ayesha in this silent-film English version of the H. Rider Haggard novel.

*She*
1935. Irving Pichel, Lansing C. Holden. United States.
An expedition team in search of the flame of eternal youth finds an immortal goddess. Hammer Studios remade the film in 1965 with Ursula Andress as Queen Ayesha.

*Single White Female*
1992. Barbet Schroeder. United States.
Bridget Fonda plays Allison who, after a falling out with her boyfriend, advertises for a roommate. The mousy girl (Jennifer Jason Leigh) who answers the ad seems perfect until, little by little, Allison figures out that her new roommate is adopting all of her mannerisms and personality traits.

*Sins of Jezebel*
1954. Reginald Le Borg. United States.
The heathen Jezebel (Paulette Goddard) marries the King of Israel, leading to the destruction of the entire kingdom.

*Sleeping Beauty*
1959. Clyde Geronimi. United States.
Sleeping Beauty is cursed by a wicked witch, and the prince who falls in love with her tries to wake her from her eternal slumber. To do so, he must do battle with Maleficent, one of the greatest of Disney's villains.

*The Snake Woman*
1961. Sidney J. Fury. England.
A doctor trying to cure his pregnant wife's illness injects her with snake venom, and she gives birth to a cold-blooded killer with the ability to turn herself into a snake.

*Snow White and the Seven Dwarves*
1937. David Hand. United States.
Another Disney classic, with Snow White as the young virgin, her wicked stepmother who is also the haggard old crone, and a magic mirror who sees and tells all.

*The Sorceress*
1988. Suzanne Schiffman. France.
A friar in medieval Europe has a spiritual crisis when he falls in love with a village healer and midwife who follows the ways of the old religion.

*Species*
1995. Roger Donaldson. United States.
An action-packed film at the center of which is an alien in the form of a beautiful young woman following an instinctual urge to procreate. Her instinct for self-preservation results in a trail of dead men who had initially seemed appropriate mates.

*Sudden Fear*
1952. David Miller. United States.
Joan Crawford is a successful playwright who falls in love and marries her newest leading man, only to find that he and his lover are planning to kill her.

*Suddenly, Last Summer*
1959. Joseph L. Mankiewicz. United States.
Katharine Hepburn is the aging mother of Sebastian, who was killed in a violent attack, and Elizabeth Taylor is the young niece who witnessed his murder, in this screen version of the Tennessee Williams play.

*Sunset Boulevard*
1950. Billy Wilder. United States.
Gloria Swanson stars as Norma Desmond, the aging movie star living in a decadent Hollywood mansion and longing for a comeback.

*Terror in the Crypt* (or *La MaldiciLn de los Karnsteins)*
1962. Camillo Mastrocinque. Spain.
It appears that the daughter of Count Karnstein has inherited the vampire curse.

*The Three Weird Sisters*
1948. Daniel Birt. England.
Three sisters plot to kill their half-brother in order to gain his inheritance.

*The Torrent*
1926. Monta Bell. United States.
Greta Garbo plays a Spanish peasant girl who becomes a famous prima donna after being deserted by her very first love.

*Touch of Evil*
1958. Orson Welles. United States.
Marlene Dietrich stars in this film about murder, kidnapping, and police corruption in a Mexican town just over the border.

*Twins of Evil*
1971. John Hough. England.
This is third in the Hammer Studios "Karnstein Trilogy." Count Karnstein and his ancestor Carmilla entice one of a set of twins into a life of debauchery and violence.

*Vamp*
1986. Richard Wenk. United States.
Three boys in search of a exotic dancer for their party stumble into the After Dark Club, which is run by the vampire Katrina (Grace Jones) and her vampiric entourage.

*The Vampire Beast Craves Blood* (also *Blood Beast Terror)*
1967. Vernon Sewell. England.
A scientist's daughter periodically turns into a moth and kills local townspeople.

*Vampire in Brooklyn*
1995. Wes Craven. United States.
Angela Bassett is the daughter of a human man and a vampire woman, one of the last of a race of vampires from ancient Africa, and Eddie Murphy is the vampire prince who must convince her that she must continue the family line.

*The Vampire Lovers*
1970. Roy Ward Baker. England.
This gothic thriller was first in the Hammer Studios "Karnstein Trilogy." Ingrid Pitt is Carmilla in this cult classic that plays up the romantic element.

*The Vampire Woman*
1962. Li Tie. Hong Kong.
A woman found sucking her infant's blood is accused of witchcraft and is buried alive.

*The Vampire of the Opera* (or *Il Vampiro dell'Opera)*
1964. Renato Polselli. Italy.
A group of actors enters a deserted opera house. A mysterious woman follows a stranger into the basement, only to return as a vampire. One by one, she seduces the women, and then the men, in the acting troupe.

*Vampirella*
1996. Roger Corman. United States.
This made-for-cable film features the buxom alien vampire of comic-book fame.

*Vampyr*
1931. Carl-Theodor Dreyer. Denmark.
A moody and atmospheric film inspired by Le Fanu's collection of short stories, *In a Glass Darkly*. The vampire hag resembles the witch of fairy tales more than the laguorous Carmilla.

*Vampyres* (also *Daughters of Dracula, Blood Hunger*, and *Satan's Daughters*)
1974. Joseph Larraz. England.
Two lesbian vampires lure unsuspecting men to their lair.

*Vampyros Lesbos*
1970. Jesus Franco. Spain.
A female descendent of Count Dracula entices young women to her lair on an isolated island.

*The Velvet Vampire*
1971. Stephanie Rothman. United States.
A bisexual vampire living in the desert lures a young couple to her home and then seduces them both.

*The Wasp Woman*
1959. Roger Corman. United States.
A cosmetics tycoon, troubled by her advancing age, develops a youth serum that turns her into a blood-thirsty insect.

*The Wasp Woman*
1996. Jim Wynorski. United States.
This is a cable remake of the 1959 B-movie.

*What Ever Happened to Baby Jane?*
1962. Robert Aldrich. United States.
Bette Davis and Joan Crawford are bitter and angry sisters, one fixated on her past as a child star (Davis) and the other confined to a wheelchair (Crawford). When Jane discovers her sister's plan for having her institutionalized, she begins to torment her, eventually leaving her to die. Davis was nominated for an Academy Award for Best Actress.

*The Wicked Lady*
1945. Leslie Arliss. England.
This film is about a scheming woman who steals her best friend's fiancé and later becomes a notorious "highwayman."

*The Wicked Lady*
1983. Michael Winner. United States.
This is a remake of the 1945 British film with Faye Dunaway, John Gielgud, Denholm Elliott, and Alan Bates. Notable for its nudity, but otherwise uninteresting.

*The Wicker Man*
1975. Robin Hardy. United States.
Christopher Lee stars in this cult classic about an British island whose population has returned to ancient pagan practices. Britt Eckland is the island's priestess who initiates the young men of the village through a fertility rite of passage.

*The Witches*
1990. Nicholas Roeg. England.
Anjelica Huston is a witch with a plan to turn all of England's children into mice, in this film based on a story by Roald Dahl.

*The Witches of Eastwick*
1987. George Miller. United States.
Cher, Michelle Pfeiffer, and Susan Sarandon are three witches who, in their search for the perfect man, inadvertently conjure the devil.

*Witness for the Prosecution*
1957. Billy Wilder. United States.
Marlene Dietrich stars as the devoted wife of Tyrone Power who has been accused of murdering an elderly woman for her money.

*The Women*
1939. George Cukor. United States.
Women gossip, rumormonger, and backbite in this comedy of manners. The all-star cast includes Norma Shearer, Rosalind Russell, Joan Fontaine, Paulette Goddard, and Joan Crawford.

*Zou Zou*
1934. Marc Allegret. France.
Josephine Baker debuts in the "talkies" as a laundress who fills in for the leading lady on opening night becomes a star.

## Video Sources

T.L.A. Video Management, Inc.
1520 Locust Street, Ste. 200
Philadelphia, PA 19102
1-800-333-8521

Video Vision
Attn: Chris Hendlin
4603 Bloomington Ave.
Minneapolis, MN 55407
612-728-0000

House of Monsters
2038 North Clark St. No. 348
Chicago, IL 60614
Fax: 312-929-7205

Video Oyster
145 W. 12th Street
New York, NY 10011
Fax: 212-989-3533

Movies Unlimited
1-800-4-Movies
Outside the United States: 215-637-4444
e-mail: movies@moviesunlimited.com

Sinister Cinema
P.O. Box 4369
Dept. F
Medford, OR 97501
541-773-6860

## Film and Video Guides

Connor, Martin and Jim Craddock. *VideoHound's Golden Movie Retriever.* Visible Ink. Detroit, MI. 1998.

Melton, J. Gordon. *VideoHound's Vampires on Video.* Visible Ink. Detroit, MI. 1997.

Murray, Raymond. *Images in the Dark: An Encyclopedia of Gay and Lesbian Film and Video.* TLA Publications. Philadelphia, PA. 1994.

Amanda Donahoe in *Lair of the White Worm* (1988).

# Index

## S



## T

## More books by Pam Keesey:

"Perfect for curling up on dark and stormy winter nights..." – The Rocket

*Dark Angels* and *Daughters Of Darkness*, Pam Keesey's bestselling lesbian vampire collections, feature the quintessential bad girls, archetypes of passion and terror. Guaranteed to get under your skin, piercing with tales of desire so sharply erotic you'll swear you've been bitten!

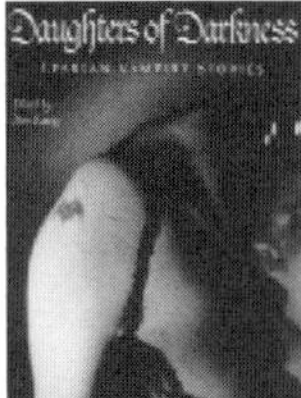


**DAUGHTERS OF DARKNESS**: Lesbian Vampire Stories
Edited by Pam Keesey
Features Katherine V. Forrest, Pat Califia, Jewelle Gomez, Robbi Sommers–as well as the most famous lesbian vampire story of all time, "Carmilla," written in 1871 by J. Sheridan LeFanu.
Bibliography and filmography
250 pages $12.95
ISBN: 0-939416-78-6

**DARK ANGELS**: Lesbian Vampire Stories
Edited by Pam Keesey
Amelia G, Gary Bowen, Melanie Tem, Cora Linn Daniels, Carol Leonard, Lawrence Schimel, Cecilia Tan, Thomas S. Roche, Renee Charles, Alejandra Pizarnik, Shawn Dell.
145 pages $10.95
ISBN: 1-57344-014-0

**WOMEN WHO RUN WITH THE WEREWOLVES**:
Tales of Blood, Lust and Metamorphosis
Edited by Pam Keesey
Ursula LeGuin, Suzy McKee Charnas, Amelia G., Thomas Roche, Lawrence Schimel, Charlee Jacob, Melanie Tem, Lawrence Schimel, Thomas Roche, Tom Piccirilli
200 pages $12.95
ISBN: 1-57344-057-4

## Other Vampires/Horror books available from Cleis Press:

**BROTHERS OF THE NIGHT**
Gay Vampire Stories
Edited by Michael Rowe and Thomas Roche
Bruce Benderson, Michael Thomas Ford, Caitlin R. Kiernan, Ron Oliver, Simon Sheppard, Robert Thompson, and more.
180 pages $14.95
ISBN: 1-57344-025-6

**SONS OF DARKNESS**
Tales of Men, Blood and Immortality
Edited by Michael Rowe and Thomas Roche
180 pages $12.95
ISBN: 1-57344-059-0

## Vampires & Horror

*Brothers of the Night: Gay Vampire Stories* edited by Michael Rowe and Thomas S. Roche. ISBN: 1-57344-025-6 14.95 paper.

*Dark Angels: Lesbian Vampire Stories,* edited by Pam Keesey. Lambda Literary Award Nominee. ISBN 1-7344-014-0 10.95 paper.

*Daughters of Darkness: Lesbian Vampire Stories,* edited by Pam Keesey. ISBN: 0-939416-78-6 12.95 paper.

*Vamps: An Illustrtated History of the Femme Fatale* by Pam Keesey. ISBN: 1-57344-026-4 21.95.

*Sons of Darkness: Tales of Men, Blood and Immortality,* edited by Michael Rowe and Thomas S. Roche. Lambda Literary Award Nominee. ISBN: 1-57344-059-0 12.95 paper.

*Women Who Run with the Werewolves: Tales of Blood, Lust and Metamorphosis,* edited by Pam Keesey. Lambda Literary Award Nominee. ISBN: 1-57344-057-4 12.95 paper.

## Gender Transgression

*Body Alchemy: Transsexual Portraits* by Loren Cameron. Lambda Literary Award Winner. ISBN: 1-57344-062-0 24.95 paper.

*Dagger: On Butch Women,* edited by Roxxie, Lily Burana, Linnea Due. ISBN: 0-939416-82-4 14.95 paper.

*I Am My Own Woman: The Outlaw Life of Charlotte von Mahlsdorf,* translated by Jean Hollander. ISBN: 1-57344-010-8 12.95 paper.

*PoMoSexuals: Challenging Assumptions about Gender and Sexuality* edited by Carol Queen and Lawrence Schimel. Preface by Kate Bornstein. ISBN: 1-57344-074-4 14.95 paper.

*Sex Changes: The Politics of Transgenderism* by Pat Califia ISBN: 1-57344-072-8 16.95 paper.

*Switch Hitters: Lesbians Write Gay Male Erotica and Gay Men Write Lesbian Erotica,* edited by Carol Queen and Lawrence Schimel. ISBN: 1-57344-021-3 12.95 paper.

## Sexual Politics

*Forbidden Passages: Writings Banned in Canada,* introductions by Pat Califia and Janine Fuller. Lambda Literary Award Winner. ISBN: 1-57344-019-1 14.95 paper.

*Public Sex: The Culture of Radical Sex* by Pat Califia. ISBN: 0-939416-89-1 12.95 paper.

*Real Live Nude Girl: Chronicles of Sex-Positive Culture* by Carol Queen. ISBN: 1-57344-073-6. 14.95 paper.

*Sex Work: Writings by Women in the Sex Industry,* edited by Frédérique Delacoste and Priscilla Alexander. ISBN: 0-939416-11-5 16.95 paper.

*Susie Bright's Sexual Reality: A Virtual Sex World Reader* by Susie Bright. ISBN: 0-939416-59-X 9.95 paper.

*Susie Bright's Sexwise* by Susie Bright. ISBN: 1-57344-002-7 10.95 paper.

*Susie Sexpert's Lesbian Sex World* by Susie Bright. ISBN: 0-939416-35-2 9.95 paper.

## Erotic Literature

*Best Gay Erotica 1998,* selected by Christopher Bram, edited by Richard Labonté. ISBN: 1-57344-031-0 14.95 paper.

*Best Gay Erotica 1997,* selected by Douglas Sadownick, edited by Richard Labonté. ISBN: 1-57344-067-1 14.95 paper.

*Best Gay Erotica 1996,* selected by Scott Heim, edited by Michael Ford. ISBN: 1-57344-052-3 12.95 paper.

*Best Lesbian Erotica 1998,* selected by Jenifer Levin, edited by Tristan Taormino. ISBN: 1-57344-032-9 14.95 paper.

## Cleis Press Books

*Best Lesbian Erotica 1997,* selected by Jewelle Gomez, edited by Tristan Taormino. ISBN: 1-57344-065-5 14.95 paper.

*Serious Pleasure: Lesbian Erotic Stories and Poetry,* edited by the Sheba Collective. ISBN: 0-939416-45-X 9.95 paper.

### Lesbian and Gay Studies

*The Case of the Good-For-Nothing Girlfriend* by Mabel Maney. Lambda Literary Award Nominee. ISBN: 0-939416-91-3 10.95 paper.

*The Case of the Not-So-Nice Nurse* by Mabel Maney. Lambda Literary Award Nominee. ISBN: 0-939416-76-X 9.95 paper.

Nancy Clue and the Hardly Boys in *A Ghost in the Closet* by Mabel Maney. Lambda Literary Award Nominee. ISBN: 1-57344-012-4 10.95 paper.

*Different Daughters: A Book by Mothers of Lesbians,* second edition, edited by Louise Rafkin. ISBN: 1-57344-050-7 12.95 paper.

*Different Mothers: Sons & Daughters of Lesbians Talk about Their Lives,* edited by Louise Rafkin. Lambda Literary Award Winner. ISBN: 0-939416-41-7 9.95 paper.

*A Lesbian Love Advisor* by Celeste West. ISBN: 0-939416-26-3 9.95 paper.

*On the Rails: A Memoir,* second edition, by Linda Niemann. Introduction by Leslie Marmon Silko. ISBN: 1-57344-064-7. 14.95 paper.

*Queer Dog: Homo Pup Poetry,* edited by Gerry Gomez Pearlberg. ISBN: 1-57344-071-X. 12.95. paper.

### Sex Guides

*Good Sex: Real Stories from Real People,* second edition, by Julia Hutton. ISBN: 1-57344-000-0 14.95 paper.

*The New Good Vibrations Guide to Sex: Tips and techniques from America's favorite* sex-toy store, second edition, by Cathy Winks and Anne Semans. ISBN: 1-57344-069-8 21.95 paper.

*The Ultimate Guide to Anal Sex for Women* by Tristan Taormino. ISBN: 1-57344-028-0 14.95 paper.

### Debut Fiction

*Memory Mambo* by Achy Obejas. Lambda Literary Award Winner. ISBN: 1-57344-017-5 12.95 paper.

*We Came All The Way from Cuba So You Could Dress Like This?: Stories* by Achy Obejas. Lambda Literary Award Nominee. ISBN: 0-939416-93-X 10.95 paper.

*Seeing Dell* by Carol Guess ISBN: 1-57344-023-X 12.95 paper.

### World Literature

*A Forbidden Passion* by Cristina Peri Rossi. ISBN: 0-939416-68-9 9.95 paper.

*Half a Revolution: Contemporary Fiction by Russian Women,* edited by Masha Gessen. ISBN 1-57344-006-X $12.95 paper.

*The Little School: Tales of Disappearance and Survival in Argentina* by Alicia Partnoy. ISBN: 0-939416-07-7 9.95 paper.

*Peggy Deery: An Irish Family at War* by Nell McCafferty. ISBN: 0-939416-39-5 9.95 paper.

### Thrillers & Dystopias

*Another Love* by Erzsébet GalgpiasSBN: 0-939416-39-5 9.95 paper.

*Dirty Weekend: A Novel of Revenge* by Helen Zahavi. ISBN: 0-939416-85-9 10.95 paper.

*Only Lawyers Dancing* by Jan McKemmish. ISBN: 0-939416-69-7 9.95 paper.

*The Wall* by Marlen Haushofer. ISBN: 0-939416-54-9 9.95 paper.

Politics of Health

*The Absence of the Dead Is Their Way of Appearing* by Mary Winfrey Trautmann. ISBN: 0-939416-04-2 8.95 paper.

*Don't: A Woman's Word* by Elly Danica. ISBN: 0-939416-22-0 8.95 paper

*Voices in the Night: Women Speaking About Incest,* edited by Toni A.H. McNaron and Yarrow Morgan. ISBN: 0-939416-02-6 9.95 paper.

*With the Power of Each Breath: A Disabled Women's Anthology,* edited by Susan Browne, Debra Connors and Nanci Stern. ISBN: 0-939416-06-9 10.95 paper.

Comix

*Dyke Strippers: Lesbian Cartoonists A to Z,* edited by Roz Warren. ISBN: 1-57344-008-6 16.95 paper.

*The Night Audrey's Vibrator Spoke: A Stonewall Riots Collection* by Andrea Natalie. Lambda Literary Award Nominee. ISBN: 0-939416-64-6 8.95 paper.

*Revenge of Hothead Paisan: Homicidal Lesbian Terrorist* by Diane DiMassa. Lambda Literary Award Nominee. ISBN: 1-57344-016-7 16.95 paper.

Travel & Cooking

*Betty and Pansy's Severe Queer Review of New York* by Betty Pearl and Pansy. ISBN: 1-57344-070-1 10.95 paper.

*Betty and Pansy's Severe Queer Review of San Francisco* by Betty Pearl and Pansy. ISBN: 1-57344-056-6 10.95 paper.

*Food for Life & Other Dish,* edited by Lawrence Schimel. ISBN: 1-57344-061-2 14.95 paper.

Writer's Reference

*Putting Out: The Essential Publishing Resource Guide For Gay and Lesbian Writers,* fourth edition, by Edisol W. Dotson. ISBN: 1-57344-033-7 14.95 paper.

Since 1980, Cleis Press has published provocative, smart books—for girlfriends of all genders. Cleis Press books are easy to find at your favorite bookstore—or direct from us! We welcome your order and will ship your books as quickly as possible. Individual orders must be prepaid (U.S. dollars only). Please add 15% shipping. CA residents add 8.5% sales tax. MasterCard and Visa orders: include account number, exp. date, and signature.

---

*How to Order*

- Phone: 1-800-780-2279 or (415) 575-4700
  Monday-Friday, 9 am-5 pm Pacific Standard Time
- Fax: (415) 575-4705
- Mail: Cleis Press P.O. Box 14684, San Francisco, California 94114
- E-mail: cleis@aol.com

Maila Nurmi as Vampira in *Plan 9 from Outer Space* (1956).